QUICK-FIX
DINNERS

QUICK-FIX
DINNERS

100+ SIMPLE RECIPES READY IN 10, 20 or 30 MINUTES

By the Editors of

Southern Living®

Oxmoor
House®

Senior Editor: Katherine Cobbs
Project Editor: Melissa Brown
Designer: Claire Cormany
Design Director: Melissa Clark
Photo Director: Paden Reich
Photographers: Daniel Agee, Caitlin Bensel, Jennifer Davick, Stephen DeVries, Laurey W. Glenn, Melina Hammer, Alison Miksch, Victor Protasio, Hector Manuel Sanchez, Time Inc. Food Studios
Prop Stylists: Kay E. Clarke, Caroline M. Cunningham, Buffy Hargett-Miller, Heather Chadduck Hillegas, Time Inc. Food Studios
Food Stylists: Marian Cooper Cairns, Vanessa Rocchio, Time Inc. Food Studios
Prop Coordinator: Audrey Davis
Assistant Production Director: Sue Chodakiewicz
Senior Production Manager: Greg A. Amason
Copy Editors: Jacqueline Giovanelli, Jasmine Hodges
Proofreader: Rebecca Brennan
Indexer: Carol Roberts
Fellows: Hailey Middlebrook, Kaitlyn Pacheco, Holly Ravazzolo, Matt Ryan, Hanna Yokeley

ISBN-13: 978-0-8487-5512-6
Library of Congress Control Number: 2017946199

First Edition 2017
Printed in the United States of America
10 9 8 7 6 5 4 3 2 1

We welcome your comments and suggestions about Time Inc. Books.

Time Inc. Books
Attention: Book Editors
P.O. Box 62310
Tampa, Florida 33662-2310

Time Inc. Books products may be purchased for business or promotional use. For information on bulk purchases, please contact Christi Crowley in the Special Sales Department at (845) 895-9858.

CONTENTS

INTRODUCTION

Busy calendars overflowing with lists of to-dos make getting a wholesome and delicious dinner on the table a constant challenge. *Southern Living* solves this problem in our test kitchens on a daily basis by creating recipes with just such schedules in mind. This book brings together some of our favorite dishes that can be prepared in either 10, 20 or 30 minutes. And we've even included a handy Month of Meals calendar to inspire different meals every night of the week for a month, so mealtime is always fresh and interesting.

There's a little something for everyone in this helpful book—whether you're trying to entice the pickiest of eaters or you love to entertain friends. On nights you have next to no time between home-from-work and the next event—there's a great selection of 10-minute recipes to get dinner on the table lightning fast. Recipe flags show busy cooks at a glance how long a dish takes from start to finish. The calendar in the front of the book indicates recipe combos that go well together so you can make a quick main dish plus a dessert, or serve a soup with that hearty salad. There are ideas for comfort foods, pasta night, and dinners to share with friends, too. *Quick-Fix Dinners* proves that dinner made fast can be flavorful, satisfying, and, best of all, stress free.

ENJOY!

A MONTH OF MEALS

	Weeknight Comfort **Monday**	**Fast & Filling** **Tuesday**	**Pasta Night** **Wednesday**
WEEK 1	Apricot-Glazed Beef Tenderloin, *page 20* ✚ Honey Custard with Berries, *page 250*	Chicken-Apple-Cheddar Sandwiches, *page 169* ✚ Apple-Cranberry Coleslaw, *page 113*	Garden Tomato Sauce over Pasta, *page 182* ✚ Choc-Cinn Latte Cake, *page 237*
WEEK 2	Pork Chops with Herb-Mustard Butter, *page 73* ✚ Snappy Pea-and-Herb Salad, *page 137*	Veggie Roll-Ups, *page 58* ✚ Berry Shortcake Ice-Cream Sandwiches, *page 238*	Chicken Pasta Primavera, *page 62* ✚ Parmesan Breadsticks, *page 149*
WEEK 3	Pan-Seared Flat Iron Steak, *page 35* ✚ Ambrosia Meringue Trifles, *page 234*	Smoked Chicken and Fontina Panini, *page 15* ✚ Spinach-Grape Chopped Salad, *page 110*	Ravioli with Butternut Cream Sauce, *page 39* ✚ Honey Custard with Berries, *page 250*
WEEK 4	Chicken and Butternut Gnocchi, *page 36* ✚ Carmelized Spicy Green Beans, *page 122*	Turkey and Ham Pine-Berry Sandwiches, *page 54* ✚ Apricot-Pistachio Cookies, *page 241*	Barbeque Mac and Cheese, *page 28* ✚ Snappy Pea-and- Herb Salad, *page 137*
WEEK 5	Chicken Bog, *page 40* ✚ Pumpkin-Gingersnap Bars, *page 249*	Smoked Paprika Salmon Sliders, *page 178* ✚ Roasted Broccoli with Orange-Chipotle Butter, *page 118*	Pasta Puttanesca, *page 161* ✚ Quick Apple Crisp, *page 242*

Soup & Salad Thursday	Dinner Party Friday
Tomato-Basil Bisque, *page 50* **+** Chicken-and-Wild Rice Salad, *page 171*	5-Ingredient Slow Cooker Pulled Pork, *page 23* **+** Creamed Silver Queen Corn, *page 141* **+** Chocolate-Pecan Butter Crunch Candy, *page 245*
Tortilla Soup, *page 24* **+** Chipotle Taco Salad, *page 93*	Buttery Garlic Shrimp, *page 209* **+** Fontina-Pesto Toasts, *page 101* **+** Loaded Bittersweet Chocolate Bark, *page 246*
Shrimp Noodle Bowl, *page 181* **+** Sesame-Chicken Garden Salad, *page 172*	Beef Fajitas with Pico de Gallo, *page 190* **+** Chipotle Taco Salad, *page 93* **+** Berry Shortcake Ice-Cream Sandwiches, *page 238*
Coconut-Corn Chowder with Chicken, *page 153* **+** Tropical Shrimp Salad, *page 98*	Kickin' Orange-Glazed Chicken, *page 66* **+** Veggie Fried Rice, *page 65* **+** Strawberry-Ginger Lemonade Floats, *page 233*
Tomato and Red Pepper Soup, *page 27* **+** Italian Salad, *page 109*	Cast-Iron Chicken Piccata, *page 225* **+** Candied Balsamic Tomatoes and Mozzarella Salad, *page 89* **+** Choc-Cinn Latte Cake, *page 237*

PREPARE IN ADVANCE:

Stock your freezer with ground beef, chicken, vegetables, etc., and your pantry with dried beans, pasta, canned tomatoes, olives, and seasonings.

CHOOSE RECIPES AND SHOP DELIBERATELY:

Choose recipes and write down the necessary ingredients before you head to the store.

COOK ONCE-EAT TWICE:

If you make a big pot of tomato soup over the weekend, make enough to last into the week. Reheat, add shredded chicken, diced sausage, or rice and you have another supper with minimal time and expense.

WORK A LITTLE NOW OR WORK MORE LATER:

Read through your recipe the night before and find ways to save time: chop veggies and store in the fridge, or blend seasoning mixes and keep on the countertop.

COMFORT FOOD CLASSICS

The soulful dishes we all love to
linger over and enjoy together
don't have to involve lots of prep or
hours of cooking in the kitchen.
These options are ready in minutes.

10
MINUTES

SMOKED CHICKEN AND FONTINA PANINI

Crusty on the outside, gooey on the inside, this sandwich requires little effort and makes a satisfying lunch or light dinner. No panini press? You can make hot sandwiches with two heavy cast-iron skillets. While you're cooking a sandwich in one skillet, heat the second one on a separate burner. Once hot, place the second skillet on top of the sandwich for 1 to 2 minutes. Repeat on the flip side, cooking for 1 to 2 minutes more.

10 MINUTES · SERVES 2

1 (8-ounce) loaf ciabatta bread, cut in half horizontally

3 tablespoons refrigerated pesto sauce

2 plum tomatoes, sliced

1 cup shredded smoked chicken

2 (1-ounce) slices fontina cheese

1. Preheat the panini press according to the manufacturer's instructions.

2. Spread the bottom half of the bread with the pesto. Top with the tomatoes, chicken, and cheese. Top with the remaining bread slice.

3. Place the sandwich in the panini press; cook 3 to 4 minutes or until the cheese melts and the bread is toasted. Cut into quarters, and serve hot.

KITCHEN SECRET: USING A PANINI PRESS

The popular Italian-style sandwiches known as panini are prepared in a special grill press that eliminates the need for turning. The top and bottom heating units cook sandwiches quickly and evenly, compressing and searing the bread to create distinctive ridges. Floating hinges on the press accommodate thick-sliced breads.

ITALIAN GRILLED CHEESE

This American classic borrows the flavors of Italy. Sun-dried tomatoes, fresh basil, and fontina cheese perk up this sandwich that you can prepare in a panini press or on a griddle like a traditional grilled cheese. Add a side salad, and you've got a meal!

10 MINUTES · SERVES 4

2 ounces thinly sliced pancetta

8 (0.8-ounce) slices Italian bread

¼ teaspoon freshly ground black pepper

4 (¾-ounce) slices fontina cheese

1¾ ounces large sun-dried tomatoes, packed without oil (about 12)

8 large fresh basil leaves

Olive oil cooking spray

1. Preheat the panini press according to the manufacturer's instructions.

2. Cook the pancetta in a large nonstick skillet over medium-high 5 minutes, turning often, until crisp. Remove the pancetta from the pan. Drain on paper towels.

3. Sprinkle 4 bread slices evenly with the pepper; top evenly with the pancetta, cheese slices, tomatoes, and basil leaves. Top the sandwiches with the remaining bread slices. Coat the outsides of the sandwiches with the cooking spray.

4. Place the sandwiches in the panini press; cook 2 minutes or until the cheese melts and the bread is toasted. Cut the sandwiches in half, if desired.

10
MINUTES

10
MINUTES

CALIFORNIA SMOKED CHICKEN SANDWICHES

This California favorite begins with shredded chicken and ends with a smoky paprika aioli. In between are creamy avocado and tomato slices. To tamp down the smokiness, use regular paprika in the aioli.

10 MINUTES · SERVES 6

12 (0.7-ounce) slices sourdough bread
Smoked Paprika Aioli
6 (¼-inch-thick) slices tomato
2 cups shredded smoked chicken
1 medium-sized ripe avocado, cut into 12 slices

1. Toast the bread. While the bread toasts, make the Smoked Paprika Aioli.

2. Spread the aioli evenly on 6 bread slices. Layer the tomato, chicken, and avocado evenly over the aioli. Top with the remaining bread slices.

SMOKED PAPRIKA AIOLI

3 tablespoons mayonnaise
1 tablespoon finely chopped scallions
1 teaspoon smoked paprika
½ teaspoon lemon zest
1 garlic clove, minced

Whisk together all the ingredients in a small bowl. Cover and chill until ready to serve. Makes ¼ cup

APRICOT-GLAZED BEEF TENDERLOIN

The tangy-sweet apricot glaze is a bright pairing for this rich cut of beef. Serve with roasted potatoes and a simple green salad.

10 MINUTES · SERVES 4

- 1 tablespoon unsalted butter
- 4 (4-ounce) beef tenderloin steaks, trimmed (about 1-inch thick)
- 1/2 teaspoon ground cumin
- 1/2 teaspoon freshly ground black pepper
- 1/4 teaspoon table salt
- 1/2 cup apricot preserves
- 2 tablespoons water

1. Melt the butter in a large nonstick skillet over medium-high.

2. While the butter melts, sprinkle the steaks evenly with the cumin, pepper, and salt. Add the steaks to the pan; Cook in the melted butter 3 minutes on each side or until desired degree of doneness. Transfer the steaks to a serving platter; keep warm. Reduce heat to medium.

3. Stir the preserves and 2 tablespoons water into the drippings, scraping the pan to loosen the browned bits. Cook, stirring constantly, over medium 1 minute or until bubbly.

4. Place 1 steak on each of 4 plates. Spoon the sauce evenly over the steaks.

10
MINUTES

SLOW
COOKER
10-MINUTE
PREP!

5-INGREDIENT SLOW-COOKER PULLED PORK

Start with a pork shoulder and you only need four more ingredients to make this great dish. You probably have chicken broth in your pantry already, so grab some onions, baby bell peppers, and the seasoning blend, and this simple dish is ready to prepare. Give it 8 to 10 hours in the slow cooker, and it will be fork-tender, ready to shred, and mouthwateringly delicious.

10-MINUTE PREP! · 8 HOURS 10 MINUTES · SERVES 8 TO 10

- 2 **large sweet onions, cut into ½-inch slices**
- 2 **red baby bell peppers, sliced**
- 2 **orange baby bell peppers, sliced**
- 1 **(5- to 6-pound) boneless pork shoulder roast (Boston butt)**
- 2 **tablespoons garlic-oregano-red pepper seasoning blend**
- 1 **teaspoon table salt**
- 1 **(10 ½-ounce) can condensed chicken broth, undiluted**
  Fresh thyme sprigs (optional)

1. Place the onion and bell pepper in a lightly greased 6-quart slow cooker. Rub the roast with the seasoning blend and salt; place the roast on the onion and bell pepper. Pour the broth over the roast. Cover and cook on LOW 8 to 10 hours or until the meat shreds easily with a fork.

2. Transfer the roast to a cutting board or serving platter; shred with 2 forks, removing any large pieces of fat. Remove the onion and bell pepper with a slotted spoon, and serve with the pork. Garnish with the thyme sprigs, if desired.

{ KITCHEN SECRET: SLOW-COOKER PREP }

Trim visible fat from meats before they go into the slow cooker. This keeps grease to a minimum in the cooking liquid and yields silky gravies and sauces.

TORTILLA SOUP

Look for Mexican tortilla soup broth on the soup aisle to jump-start flavor. Rotisserie chicken is another easy way to save time while adding lots of depth.

20 MINUTES · MAKES 6 QUARTS

1 (2-pound) whole rotisserie chicken

3 (10-ounce) cans mild diced tomatoes with green chiles

2 (32-ounce) containers Mexican tortilla soup broth

1 tablespoon ground cumin

1 tablespoon smoked paprika

1/2 teaspoon table salt, plus more to taste

Toppings: crisp tortilla strips, queso fresco, sliced avocado, fresh cilantro sprigs, lime wedges, sliced peppers

1. Remove the skin from the chicken, and discard; shred the meat to measure about 4 cups.

2. Bring the chicken, tomatoes, and the next 4 ingredients to a boil in a Dutch oven over medium-high. Reduce heat, cover, and simmer 15 minutes. Add the salt to taste. Serve with the desired toppings.

20
MINUTES

20
MINUTES

20
MINUTES

THE ULTIMATE GRILLED CHEESE

Using mayonnaise instead of butter adds flavor and keeps the bread from burning.

20 MINUTES · SERVES 4

- ¼ cup mayonnaise
- 8 (2-ounce) slices Italian bread
- 8 (1-ounce) slices American cheese

1. Spread 1 ½ teaspoons of the mayonnaise on 1 side of each bread slice.

2. Heat a large nonstick skillet over medium. Place 2 bread slices, mayonnaise side down, in the pan; top each with 2 cheese slices and 1 bread slice, mayonnaise sides up. Cook 3 minutes on each side or until golden brown. Repeat with the remaining bread slices and cheese.

TOMATO AND RED PEPPER SOUP

Red pepper adds a tangy zest to this classic crowd-pleaser.

20 MINUTES · SERVES 4 TO 6

- 1 (28-ounce) can whole tomatoes
- 1 (12-ounce) jar roasted red peppers, drained
- ¼ cup half-and-half
- 1 ½ teaspoons table salt
- 1 teaspoon sugar
- ½ teaspoon freshly ground black pepper
- 2 garlic cloves
- ¼ cup water
- Fresh basil leaves (optional)

Process all the ingredients in a food processor until smooth, stopping to scrape down the sides as needed. Transfer the mixture to a medium saucepan, and cook over medium–high, stirring often, 8 minutes or until hot. Serve immediately. Garnish with the basil leaves, if desired.

BARBECUE MAC AND CHEESE

Undercook the pasta by 1 minute. It will continue to cook in the creamy sauce while the crumb topping toasts under the broiler. A drizzle of barbecue sauce adds tang.

20 MINUTES · SERVES 6 TO 8

1/4 cup plus 1 1/2 teaspoons table salt

4 quarts water

1 quart milk

6 tablespoons (3 ounces) unsalted butter, cut into pieces

6 tablespoons all-purpose flour

1 pound uncooked pasta (such as penne, cavatappi, or rotini)

1 (8-ounce) package shredded extra-sharp Cheddar cheese

1 (8-ounce) package shredded Gouda cheese

1 teaspoon hot sauce (such as Tabasco)

1/2 teaspoon freshly ground black pepper

1 1/2 cups crumbled cornbread

2 teaspoons olive oil

1 pound pulled pork barbecue (without sauce)

1/2 cup chopped scallions

1/2 cup bottled barbecue sauce

1. Preheat the broiler with the oven rack 8 to 9 inches from the heat.

2. Bring 1/4 cup of the salt and 4 quarts water to a boil in a covered large Dutch oven over high.

3. While the water comes to a boil, microwave the milk in a microwave-safe 1-quart glass measuring cup covered with plastic wrap at HIGH 3 minutes. While the milk is heating, melt the butter in a 12-inch cast-iron skillet over medium. Reduce heat to medium-low; add the flour, and cook, whisking constantly, 2 minutes. Gradually whisk in the hot milk. Increase heat to medium-high, and bring to a low boil, whisking often.

4. Add the pasta to the boiling water; cook 8 minutes.

5. While the pasta cooks, continue to cook the sauce, whisking often, 6 minutes. Remove from heat; whisk in the cheeses, hot sauce, remaining 1 1/2 teaspoons salt, and pepper. Cover.

6. Stir together the cornbread and olive oil.

7. Drain the pasta, and fold into the cheese sauce. Stir in the pulled pork barbecue. Sprinkle with the cornbread mixture; sprinkle the scallions over the cornbread mixture.

8. Broil 1 to 2 minutes or until the breadcrumbs are golden brown. Drizzle with the barbecue sauce. Serve immediately.

20
MINUTES

20 MINUTES

MUSHROOM STROGANOFF

Smoked paprika adds depth to this rich and creamy meatless
main dish that gets lots of umami flavor from earthy mushrooms.

20 MINUTES · SERVES 4

- 1 (8-ounce) package egg noodles
- 1 tablespoon olive oil
- 2 tablespoons unsalted butter
- 2 (8-ounce) packages sliced cremini mushrooms
- 2 garlic cloves, minced
- 2 thyme sprigs
- 1½ teaspoons smoked paprika
- 1 teaspoon table salt
- ½ teaspoon freshly ground black pepper
- 2 tablespoons all-purpose flour
- 1½ cups chicken broth (such as Swanson)
- 1 cup sour cream
- 1 tablespoon chopped fresh flat-leaf parsley

1. Cook the egg noodles according to the package directions. Remove from heat, drain, and cover to keep warm.

2. Heat the olive oil and 1 tablespoon of the butter in a large skillet over medium-high. Add the mushrooms, and cook 5 minutes. Stir in the garlic and the next 4 ingredients, and cook, stirring occasionally, 3 minutes or until the mushrooms are slightly browned.

3. Add the flour and remaining 1 tablespoon butter, and cook, stirring constantly, 2 minutes. Whisk in the broth, and bring to a boil, whisking constantly; boil, whisking constantly, 5 minutes. Remove from heat. Stir in the sour cream and parsley, and serve over the noodles.

EASY SKILLET CORDON BLEU

This simple spin on the classic "blue ribbon" chicken dish minimizes prep by topping the breaded chicken with what are typically fillings, shaving off considerable hands-on time, but none of the rich flavor.

20 MINUTES · SERVES 4 TO 6

½ cup Italian-seasoned breadcrumbs

1 teaspoon freshly ground black pepper

½ teaspoon table salt

8 chicken tenders (about 1 pound)

1 tablespoon unsalted butter

1 tablespoon olive oil

8 slices Canadian bacon, cut into thin strips

4 (1-ounce) slices Swiss cheese, halved

Chopped fresh flat-leaf parsley leaves (optional)

1. Preheat the broiler with the oven rack 5½ inches from heat.

2. Combine the breadcrumbs, pepper, and salt in a large ziplock plastic freezer bag. Rinse the chicken tenders, and add to the freezer bag. Seal the bag, and shake to coat.

3. Melt the butter with the oil in an ovenproof skillet over medium. Add the chicken to the pan; cook 3½ to 4 minutes on each side or until done. Arrange the Canadian bacon strips over the chicken in the pan, and top each tender with 1 cheese slice half. Broil 2 minutes or until the cheese is melted. Garnish with the parsley, if desired.

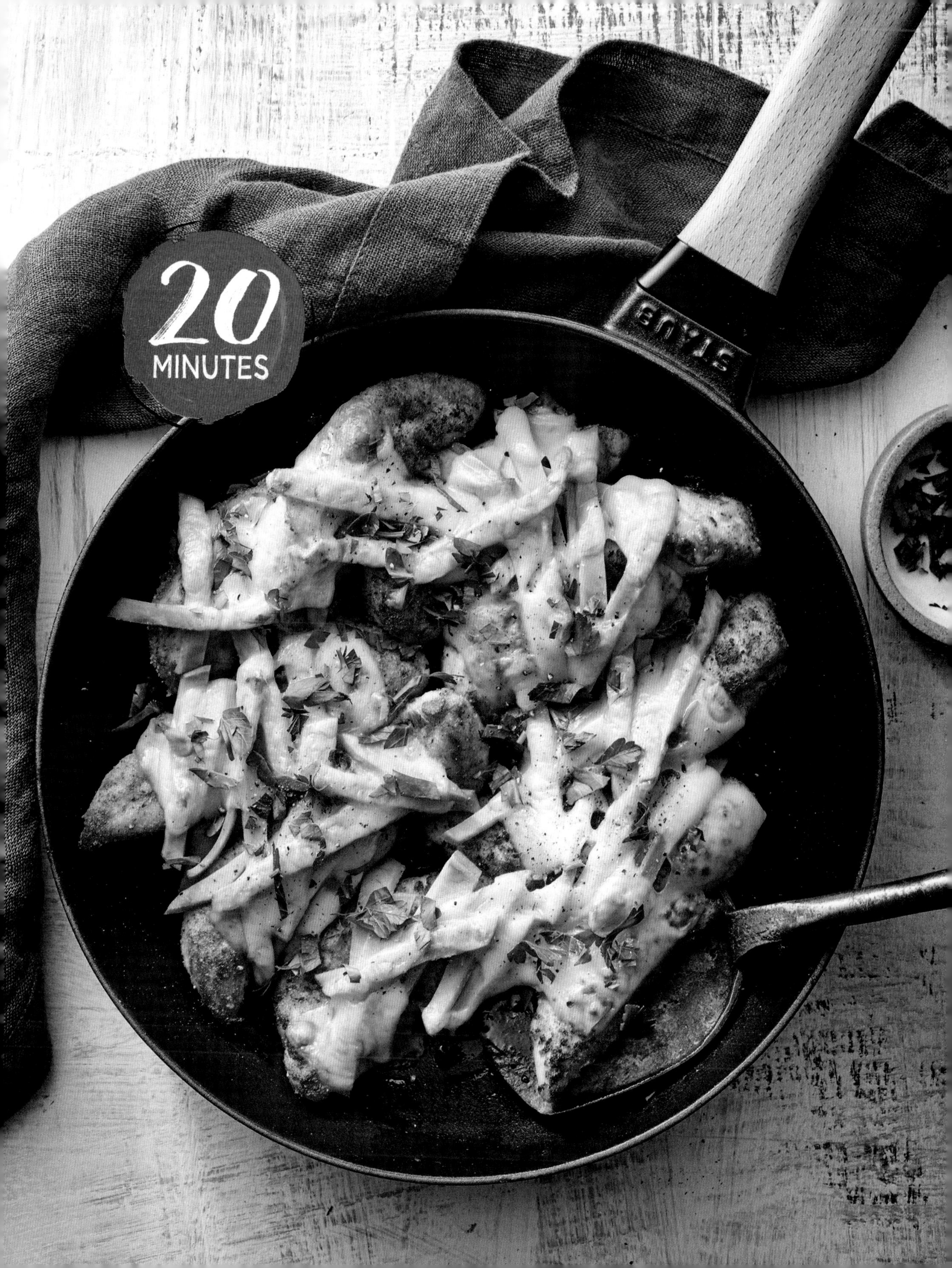
20
MINUTES

20
MINUTES

PAN-SEARED FLAT IRON STEAK

The trick to a great crust on this flat iron steak is to use a very hot skillet; a large cast-iron or heavy stainless steel skillet works best. Have your hood fan on high—there will be some smoke. If you can't find flat iron steak in your local market, a top blade chuck or sirloin steak will work just fine.

20 MINUTES · SERVES 4

1 (1-pound) flat iron steak
2 teaspoons Montreal steak seasoning
1/4 teaspoon table salt
1 tablespoon vegetable oil

1. Rub the steak evenly with the steak seasoning and salt.

2. Heat the oil in a large skillet over high. Add the steak; cook in the hot oil 4 to 5 minutes on each side or to desired degree of doneness. Let stand 5 minutes. Cut diagonally across the grain into thin strips.

WINTER VEGETABLES AND GNOCCHI

Pillowy store-bought gnocchi are a great stand-in for dumplings in this easy and comforting dish. Buy precut butternut squash, but slice any large pieces in half to ensure that it cooks evenly.

30 MINUTES · SERVES 4

1 (12 ounces) package pre-chopped fresh butternut squash

8 ounces cremini mushrooms, halved

1 cup frozen pearl onions, thawed

2 tablespoons extra-virgin olive oil

1½ teaspoons kosher salt

¼ teaspoon black pepper

1 (16 ounces) package potato gnocchi (such as Gia Russa)

2 tablespoons salted butter, softened

2 ounces Parmigiano-Reggiano cheese, shredded (about ½ cup), divided

Chopped fresh flat-leaf parsley (optional)

1. Toss together the butternut squash, mushrooms, pearl onions, olive oil, salt, and pepper. Spoon the vegetable mixture into a lightly greased 13- x 9-inch baking pan; place the pan in the oven. Preheat the oven to 450°F, leaving the pan in the oven as it preheats. Bake the vegetable mixture until the squash is tender and browned, about 20 minutes.

2. While the vegetables bake, prepare the gnocchi according to the package directions, reserving 1 cup of the cooking water.

3. Remove the vegetable mixture from the oven. Stir in the gnocchi and the softened butter. (Be careful—the pan will be hot.) Gradually add up to 1 cup of the reserved cooking water, ¼ cup at a time, stirring until a slightly thick sauce begins to form. Stir in ¼ cup of the shredded cheese. Sprinkle top with remaining ¼ cup cheese. Divide the vegetable and dumpling mixture evenly among 4 bowls. Garnish with the chopped parsley, if desired, and serve immediately.

30
MINUTES

30
MINUTES

RAVIOLI WITH BUTTERNUT CREAM SAUCE

A creamy butternut squash, brown butter, and sage sauce livens up frozen cheese-filled ravioli. A quick visit under the broiler just before serving, and the end result is crispy perfection.

30 MINUTES · SERVES 6

1 (22-ounce) package frozen cheese ravioli (such as Celentano)

Butternut Squash Cream Sauce

2 tablespoons unsalted butter

12 sage leaves

3 ounces shredded 4-cheese Italian blend cheese (about 3/4 cup)

Fresh sage leaves (optional)

1. Preheat the broiler.

2. Cook the ravioli according to the package directions, omitting salt and fat. Drain.

3. While the ravioli cooks, make the Butternut Squash Cream Sauce.

4. Divide the ravioli evenly among 6 greased shallow baking dishes. Spoon the cream sauce evenly over the ravioli in the dishes.

5. Melt the butter in a large nonstick skillet over medium-high. Add the sage; sauté 3 minutes or until the bubbles subside and the butter begins to brown. Drizzle the butter mixture evenly over the sauce. Sprinkle evenly with the cheese.

6. Place the dishes on a large rimmed baking sheet. Broil 3 minutes or until the cheese melts and begins to brown. Garnish with the sage leaves, if desired.

BUTTERNUT SQUASH CREAM SAUCE

1/2 cup chopped toasted walnuts

1/2 cup organic vegetable stock

3 ounces cream cheese (about 6 tablespoons)

1 tablespoon chopped fresh chives

2 garlic cloves, minced

1/2 teaspoon orange zest

1/4 teaspoon table salt

1/4 teaspoon freshly ground black pepper

1 (12-ounce) package frozen butternut squash puree, thawed

Process all the ingredients in a food processor until smooth. Makes about 2 1/2 cups

CHICKEN BOG

A distant cousin of Low Country pilau, Chicken Bog highlights the best qualities of both chicken and rice. The chicken is juicy, and the rice absorbs the flavorful chicken juices and seasonings. In the best Southern rice preparations, the grains don't stick together. Some people theorize that Chicken Bog gets its name because the chicken is bogged in rice.

30 MINUTES · SERVES 4

2 tablespoons olive oil

1 cup chopped yellow onion

1 cup chopped carrots (about 3 carrots)

2 teaspoons chopped garlic

1½ cups uncooked long-grain white rice

1 teaspoon table salt

¾ teaspoon freshly ground black pepper

4 cups chicken stock

1 (4-inch) piece Parmesan cheese rind

4 cups shredded rotisserie chicken (about 1 rotisserie chicken)

3 tablespoons chopped fresh flat-leaf parsley

1 tablespoon fresh lemon juice

1½ ounces Parmesan cheese, shaved (about ⅓ cup)

1. Heat the oil in a Dutch oven over medium-high. Add the onion and carrots, and cook, stirring occasionally, until beginning to soften, about 4 minutes. Add the garlic, rice, salt, and pepper, and cook until fragrant and the rice begins to toast, about 3 minutes.

2. Stir in the stock, and add the Parmesan rind; bring to a boil. Reduce heat to low. Cover and simmer until the rice is just cooked through, about 18 minutes. Uncover and discard the rind; stir in the chicken. Cook until the chicken is heated through, about 5 minutes.

3. Stir in the parsley and lemon juice just before serving, and top with the shaved Parmesan.

KITCHEN SECRET: SAY "CHEESE!"

After grating a fresh wedge of Parmesan cheese down to its rind, don't toss it. Freeze the rind in a ziplock freezer bag. It will add rich flavor to simmering soups, stews, and sauces.

30
MINUTES

30
MINUTES

SAUSAGE, MUSHROOM, AND COLLARDS PASTA

Cooking the entire recipe in one pan—including the noodles—allows the pasta starch to thicken the cooking liquid, making a rich sauce without butter or cream. Be sure to use a large, high-sided skillet so you can easily simmer and stir the pasta. We paired the pasta with chicken sausage, mushrooms, red onion, and collard greens, but you can substitute other types of sausage and vegetables. Try different shapes of dried pasta such as ziti, fusilli, or even linguine. (Skip the thin spaghetti or angel hair pasta; a thicker noodle works best here.)

30 MINUTES · SERVES 4

2 teaspoons olive oil

12 ounces fully cooked sweet Italian-style chicken sausage (such as Al Fresco), cut into ¼-inch-thick slices

1 pound cremini mushrooms, sliced

4 cups unsalted chicken stock

½ teaspoon table salt

4 cups chopped, stemmed collard greens (about 3 ounces)

10 ounces uncooked penne pasta

1 cup thinly sliced red onion

1 tablespoon thinly sliced garlic

1 tablespoon red wine vinegar

½ teaspoon crushed red pepper

1. Heat the oil in a large, high-sided skillet over medium-high. Add the sausage and mushrooms; cook, stirring often, until browned, about 8 minutes.

2. Add the stock and the next 5 ingredients; bring to a boil. Cook, stirring constantly, until the pasta is al dente and the liquid is mostly absorbed, about 15 minutes.

3. Stir in the vinegar, and sprinkle with the crushed red pepper.

SALSA VERDE CORN CHIP PIE

Make this Texas Friday-night-football favorite your any-weeknight supper. It's an easy on-the-go meal that can be eaten right out of the bag. Just heap the toppings inside.

30 MINUTES · SERVES 6

5   teaspoons olive oil

2   cups frozen whole kernel yellow corn, thawed

1   (9-ounce) package garlic pork sausage links, casings removed

1   medium-sized sweet onion, chopped

2   teaspoons chili powder

1   teaspoon ground cumin

1   (16-ounce) bottle salsa verde

2   (4.5-ounce) cans chopped green chiles

1   (16-ounce) can navy beans, drained and rinsed

2   tablespoons fresh lime juice

6   cups original flavor corn chips

4   ounces shredded pepper Jack cheese (about 1 cup)

Toppings: fresh cilantro leaves, sliced radishes, sliced avocado, lime wedges

1. Heat 1 tablespoon of the oil in a large skillet over medium. Add the corn to the oil; sauté in the oil 3 to 4 minutes or until the corn begins to char. Remove the corn from the skillet.

2. Increase heat to medium–high, and sauté the sausage 6 to 8 minutes or until browned. Remove from the skillet, and drain on paper towels.

3. Heat the remaining 2 teaspoons oil in the skillet over medium–high; sauté the onion in the oil 4 to 5 minutes or until tender. Stir in the chili powder and cumin; cook, stirring often, 2 to 3 minutes. Reduce heat to medium, and stir in the salsa, chiles, and sausage. Cook, stirring often, 7 to 8 minutes or until slightly thickened. Remove from heat; stir in the beans, lime juice, and corn.

4. Divide the chips evenly among 6 plates. Spoon the sausage mixture over the chips; top with half of the cheese. Serve with the toppings and the remaining cheese.

30
MINUTES

SKILLET SHRIMP CHILAQUILES

Crisp, freshly fried tortilla chips are the star of this dish, and they are so easy to make at home. Cool to room temperature, about 10 minutes. Then try not to eat them all before you make these tasty shrimp chilaquiles.

30 MINUTES · SERVES 4

Vegetable or canola oil

12 (6 1/2-inch) corn tortillas

1 1/2 teaspoons table salt

2 1/2 cups green chile salsa

1 pound peeled and deveined raw medium shrimp

1/2 tablespoon ancho chile powder

2 ounces queso fresco (fresh Mexican cheese), crumbled (about 1/2 cup)

1 avocado, diced

1/4 cup packed cilantro leaves

1. Preheat the oven to 400°F. Pour the oil to a depth of 2 inches in a Dutch oven; heat the oil over medium-high to 350°F. Stack the tortillas; cut the stack into quarters to create 48 tortilla wedges. Fry the wedges, 12 at a time, in the hot oil until lightly browned, about 1 1/2 minutes per side. Quickly remove the tortilla chips from the oil, and drain on paper towels. Sprinkle the chips evenly with 3/4 teaspoon of the salt. Cool to room temperature.

2. Arrange half of the chips in a 10-inch cast-iron skillet, and pour 1/2 cup salsa over the chips. Top with the remaining chips and 2 cups salsa. Cover the pan with heavy-duty aluminum foil, and bake 15 minutes.

3. While the chips bake, toss the shrimp with the ancho chile powder and the remaining 3/4 teaspoon salt.

4. Remove the pan from the oven, and increase the oven temperature to broil. Remove and discard the foil. Arrange the shrimp on top of the tortilla mixture. Return to the oven, and broil just until the shrimp turn pink, 3 to 5 minutes.

5. Top with the queso fresco, avocado, and cilantro. Serve immediately.

PICKY
EATERS

Say goodbye to the constant conundrum
of what to cook for the hard-to-please.
These kitchen-tested favorites,
tailor-made for finicky eaters, can
be on the table in no time.

TOMATO-BASIL BISQUE

Canned tomato soup gets a boost in this satisfying version gussied up
with fresh basil, buttermilk, and a dose of spice. Serve warm or cold.

10 MINUTES · SERVES 4 TO 6

2 (10 3/4-ounce) cans tomato soup,
   undiluted

1 (14 1/2-ounce) can diced tomatoes

2 1/2 cups buttermilk

2 tablespoons chopped fresh basil

1/4 teaspoon freshly ground black pepper

1/8 teaspoon ground red pepper

Toppings: fresh basil leaves,
freshly ground black pepper,
shaved Parmesan cheese

Cook the first 6 ingredients in a 3-quart saucepan over medium, stirring often, 6 to 8 minutes or until thoroughly heated. Serve immediately with desired toppings.

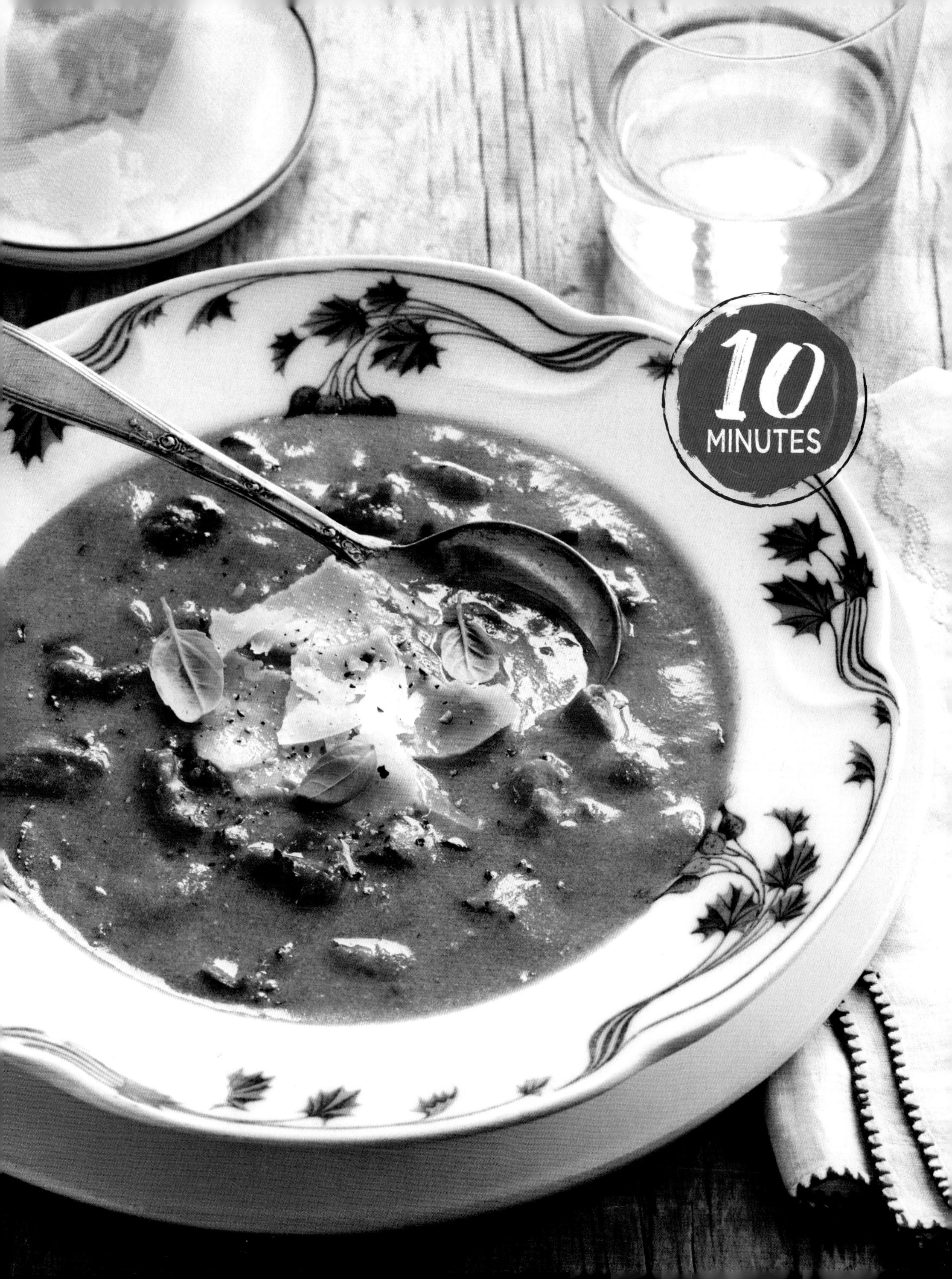
10
MINUTES

TURKEY-AND-HAM ROLL-UPS

Packaged items like flavored cream cheese and seasoned
deli meats pack in the flavor with minimal effort.

10 MINUTES · SERVES 12

- 1 cup garlic-and-herb cheese spread (such as Boursin)
- 1/2 cup chopped roasted red bell peppers
- 6 (8-inch) flour tortillas
- 3 cups firmly packed baby spinach leaves
- 12 ounces sliced deli ham
- 12 ounces sliced pepper turkey breast

Stir together the cream cheese and peppers until smooth. Spread the cream cheese mixture evenly over each tortilla. Place 1/2 cup spinach on each tortilla. Top evenly with the ham and turkey slices. Roll up, jelly-roll fashion, and cut in half. Secure each half with a wooden pick.

TURKEY AND HAM PINE-BERRY SANDWICHES

Sweet raisin bread pairs deliciously with a sandwich
filling of pineapple, ham, turkey, and cranberry relish.

10 MINUTES · SERVES 6

1 (3-ounce) package cream cheese,
softened

1/3 cup drained crushed pineapple

12 (1-ounce) slices raisin bread

1 (6-ounce) package sliced smoked
turkey breast

6 tablespoons cranberry-orange relish,
drained

1 (6-ounce) package sliced cooked ham

Stir together the cream cheese and pineapple.
Spread 2 teaspoons of the cream cheese mixture
on each bread slice. Top 6 bread slices with the
turkey. Spread the relish over the turkey slices.
Top with the ham and the remaining bread slices.

KITCHEN SECRET: JUICY FRUIT

Save the pineapple juice from canned pineapple
to keep cut fruit such as apples and bananas
from discoloring. Just toss the cut fruit in the juice,
and then discard the juice.

10
MINUTES

10 MINUTES

WAFFLED HAWAIIAN SANDWICHES

Turn up the flavor and the fun with this tropical twist on a ham and provolone sandwich with a checkerboard look. Serve with carrot sticks or other favorite veggies on the side.

10 MINUTES · SERVES 4

8 ounces shaved lower-sodium deli smoked ham

4 (1-ounce) slices reduced-fat provolone cheese

4 (1-ounce) slices fresh pineapple

8 (0.9-ounce) slices white-wheat bread
Butter-flavored cooking spray

1. Preheat a waffle iron.

2. Layer the ham, cheese, and pineapple slices evenly on 4 bread slices; top with the remaining bread slices. Coat the sandwiches and waffle iron with the cooking spray. Place the sandwiches in the waffle iron, in batches if necessary, and cook 4 to 6 minutes or until the cheese melts and the bread is toasted.

VEGGIE ROLL-UPS

Bacon adds a little slice of heaven to these quick roll-ups.
And let's face it: Bacon makes just about any sandwich better.

10 MINUTES · SERVES 4

Carrot–Red Onion Toss

½ cup refrigerated hummus

4 (8-inch) whole-wheat flour tortillas

4 slices precooked bacon

½ cup finely chopped cucumber

1. Make the Carrot–Red Onion Toss.

2. Spread the hummus evenly over the tortillas. Microwave the bacon slices according to the package directions; crumble the bacon. Sprinkle the bacon evenly over the hummus. Top evenly with the Carrot–Red Onion Toss and the cucumber; roll up.

CARROT–RED ONION TOSS

1 cup matchstick-cut carrots

⅓ cup vertically sliced red onion

2 tablespoons light red wine vinaigrette

¼ teaspoon freshly ground black pepper

Combine all the ingredients in a medium bowl; toss gently. Makes 1 ¼ cups

10
MINUTES

10
MINUTES

CHICKEN PASTA PRIMAVERA

Zesty Italian seasoning, brightly colored vegetables, and nutty-flavored Parmigiano-Reggiano cheese perfume this Italian classic.

10 MINUTES · SERVES 4

6   ounces uncooked fusilli (short twisted pasta)

3/4   pound frozen chicken thigh strips, thawed

1   teaspoon salt-free Italian medley seasoning blend (such as Mrs. Dash)

1   tablespoon olive oil

1   cup refrigerated tricolor bell pepper strips

1   (12-ounce) package fresh-cut vegetable stir-fry with broccoli, carrots, red cabbage, and snow peas (such as Eat Smart)

1/4   cup dry white wine

1.3   ounces Parmigiano-Reggiano cheese, grated (about 1/3 cup)

1/2   teaspoon freshly ground black pepper

1/4   teaspoon table salt

3   tablespoons thinly sliced fresh basil

1. Cook the pasta according to the package directions; drain.

2. While the pasta cooks, sprinkle the chicken with the Italian seasoning blend. Heat a large nonstick skillet over medium-high until hot; add 2 teaspoons of the oil. Add the chicken to the pan; sauté 4 minutes or until the chicken is done and is lightly browned.

3. Remove the chicken from the pan. Add the remaining 1 teaspoon oil to the pan. Add the bell pepper and vegetable stir-fry. Stir-fry over medium-high 3 minutes or just until the vegetables are almost tender. Stir in the wine. Stir in the hot pasta. Add the cheese, black pepper, salt, and chicken; toss well. Divide the pasta mixture evenly among 4 plates, and sprinkle evenly with the basil.

SPEEDY BLACK BEANS AND MEXICAN RICE

This hearty rice and bean dish is the perfect answer for a meatless main-dish choice and doubles perfectly.

10 MINUTES · SERVES 2

1 (8.8-ounce) pouch ready-to-serve Mexican rice
1 (15-ounce) can black beans, drained and rinsed
1 (4.4-ounce) can chopped green chiles
2 tablespoons chopped fresh cilantro
Toppings: sour cream, salsa, diced tomato, shredded Cheddar cheese, sliced scallions, cilantro leaves

1. Cook the rice according to the package directions.

2. Combine the black beans and green chiles in a microwave-safe bowl. Microwave at HIGH 90 seconds. Stir in the rice and cilantro. Serve immediately with the desired toppings.

NOTE: *We used Rice-A-Roni Express Heat & Serve Mexican Rice.*

MEXICAN BEEF 'N' RICE

Substitute 1 pound cooked lean ground beef for the black beans. Substitute 1 cup salsa for the green chiles. Prepare the recipe as directed, omitting the toppings. Serve with corn chips or in lettuce leaves, if desired. Serves 4

10
Minutes

20 Minutes

VEGGIE FRIED RICE

Instead of Chinese takeout, make this colorful
vegetable fried rice at home in a flavorful flash.

20 MINUTES · SERVES 4

1 (5.3-ounce) pouch ready-to-serve
   brown rice

1 (8-ounce) package fresh sugar
   snap peas

4 scallions, cut into 2-inch pieces

½ cup matchstick-cut carrots

1 tablespoon grated fresh ginger

2 garlic cloves, minced

2 large eggs, lightly beaten

3 tablespoons reduced-sodium
   soy sauce

2 teaspoons dark sesame oil

1. Cook the rice according to the package directions; drain well.

2. Sauté the peas, scallions, and carrots in a large nonstick skillet coated with cooking spray over medium-high 3 minutes or until crisp-tender. Add the ginger and garlic; sauté 1 minute. Add the rice, and cook 2 minutes or until thoroughly heated. Push the rice mixture to the sides of pan, making a well in the center of the mixture.

3. Add the eggs to the center of the mixture, and cook, stirring occasionally, 1 to 2 minutes or until set. Stir the eggs into the rice mixture. Stir in the soy sauce and sesame oil.

KICKIN' ORANGE-GLAZED CHICKEN

Amplify zesty flavors with a citrus glaze spiked with Dijon
and red pepper for a superfast chicken dinner tonight.

20 MINUTES · SERVES 4

- 4 (5- to 6-ounce) chicken cutlets
- 1/2 teaspoon table salt
- 1/4 teaspoon freshly ground black pepper
- 1 tablespoon butter
- 1 tablespoon olive oil
- 1/2 cup orange marmalade
- 4 teaspoons Dijon mustard
- 1 teaspoon lemon zest, plus 2 teaspoons fresh lemon juice
- 1/4 teaspoon crushed red pepper
  Lemon wedges (optional)

1. Preheat the broiler with the oven rack 8 inches from the heat. Sprinkle both sides of the cutlets with the salt and pepper. Melt the butter with the oil in a large ovenproof skillet over medium-high. Add the cutlets to the pan. Cook in the butter mixture until lightly browned, 1 to 2 minutes on each side. Tilt the pan; add the marmalade and the next 4 ingredients to the drippings, and stir until combined. Spoon the sauce over the cutlets.

2. Broil until the chicken is glazed and cooked through, about 6 minutes, turning the cutlets every minute and basting with the pan sauce. Spoon the sauce over the chicken. Garnish with the lemon wedges, if desired.

20
MINUTES

20
MINUTES

HAM STEAK WITH PINEAPPLE SALSA

Even the pickiest eaters appreciate the sweet pineapple–smoky ham flavor of this Hawaiian luau–inspired main course. Serve with steamed white rice and a side salad to round out the meal.

20 MINUTES · SERVES 4

- 1 (15 1/4-ounce) can pineapple tidbits in juice, undrained
- 1/3 cup chopped scallions
- 1 medium-sized red bell pepper, diced
- 2 tablespoons brown sugar
- 1 tablespoon cider vinegar
- 2 teaspoons reduced-sodium soy sauce
- 2 garlic cloves, minced
- 3/4 pound reduced-fat, lower-salt ham steak
- Fresh cilantro leaves (optional)

1. Drain the pineapple, reserving the juice. Combine the pineapple, 2 tablespoons of the pineapple juice, scallions, and the next 5 ingredients in a bowl; stir well.

2. Preheat the grill to medium-high (350° to 400°F).

3. Coat the grill rack with cooking spray, and place on the grill. Place the ham steak on the rack, and grill, uncovered, about 4 minutes on each side, basting often with the remaining pineapple juice. Serve the ham steak with the pineapple salsa. Garnish with the cilantro leaves, if desired.

SPICY-SWEET RIBS AND BEANS

For tender, flavorful ribs, fast-and-easy prep followed by ample hands-off time in a slow cooker is all you need. Serve with cornbread and a side of slaw for a 'cue plate any smokehouse would be proud to serve.

20-MINUTE PREP! · 7 HOURS 20 MINUTES · SERVES 8

4 pounds country-style pork ribs, trimmed
1 teaspoon garlic powder
½ teaspoon table salt
½ teaspoon freshly ground black pepper
1 (10.5-ounce) jar red pepper jelly
1 (18-ounce) bottle hickory-flavored barbecue sauce
1 medium onion, chopped
2 (16-ounce) cans pinto beans, drained and rinsed

1. Preheat the broiler with the oven rack 5 ½ inches from the heat. Cut the ribs apart; sprinkle evenly with the garlic powder, salt, and pepper. Place the ribs in a single layer in an aluminum foil–lined broiler pan.

2. Broil 9 to 10 minutes on each side or until browned.

3. Whisk together the jelly and barbecue sauce in a small bowl until blended.

4. Combine the ribs, jelly mixture, and onion in a 5-quart slow cooker. Cover and cook on LOW 6 hours; add the beans, cover, and cook 1 more hour. Remove the ribs, and drain the bean mixture, reserving the sauce. Skim the fat from the sauce. Transfer the bean mixture to a serving platter, and top with the ribs. Serve with the sauce.

SLOW COOKER
20-MINUTE PREP!

20
MINUTES

PORK CHOPS WITH HERB-MUSTARD BUTTER

A tiny dose of fresh sage blended into a sweet, creamy, mustard-spiked compound butter elevates the humble pork chop to star status.

20 MINUTES · SERVES 4

4 (1/2-inch-thick) bone-in pork loin chops

1 teaspoon table salt

1/2 teaspoon freshly ground black pepper

1/4 cup (2 ounces) butter, softened

1/4 cup chopped fresh flat-leaf parsley

2 tablespoons honey mustard

1 teaspoon chopped fresh sage
Chopped fresh flat-leaf parsley leaves (optional)

1. Preheat the broiler with the oven rack 5 inches from the heat. Sprinkle the chops evenly with the salt and pepper, and place on a wire rack in an aluminum foil-lined broiler pan.

2. Stir together the butter and the next 3 ingredients in a small bowl until blended. Top each chop with 1 rounded tablespoon of the butter mixture.

3. Broil 8 to 10 minutes or until a meat thermometer inserted into the thickest portion registers 155°F. Garnish with the parsley, if desired.

CRUNCHY CAJUN-SPICED TILAPIA

Sprinkle budget-friendly tilapia fillets with Cajun (or Creole) seasoning, dredge in flour and cornmeal, and panfry for a quick-cooking weeknight meal.

20 MINUTES · SERVES 4

4 (4- to 6-ounce) tilapia fillets
1 1/2 teaspoons Cajun seasoning*
3 tablespoons self-rising flour
1/2 cup plain yellow cornmeal
1 tablespoon butter
2 tablespoons olive oil
Lemon (optional)
Fresh flat-leaf parsley sprigs (optional)

1. Sprinkle the fillets with 1 teaspoon of the seasoning. Combine the remaining 1/2 teaspoon seasoning, flour, and cornmeal. Dredge the fillets in the flour mixture, shaking off excess.

2. Melt the butter with the oil in a large skillet over medium-high; add the fillets, and cook 3 to 4 minutes on each side or until the fish flakes with a fork. If desired, squeeze the juice from the lemon over the fillets, and garnish with the parsley. Serve immediately.

*Creole seasoning may be substituted.

CAJUN-SEASONED PAN-FRIED CHICKEN BREASTS

Substitute 4 (8-ounce) skinned and boned chicken breasts for the tilapia. Proceed with the recipe as directed, cooking 8 to 10 minutes on each side or until done.

CAJUN-SEASONED PAN-FRIED PORK CHOPS

Substitute 4 (8-ounce) bone-in center-cut pork chops for the tilapia. Proceed with the recipe as directed, cooking 8 to 10 minutes on each side or until done.

30
MINUTES

SPINACH-RAVIOLI LASAGNA

This top-rated spinach-ravioli lasagna uses convenience items, like store-bought pesto, jarred Alfredo sauce, and frozen cheese-filled ravioli, to deliver a delicious main dish with little time and effort on your part.

30 MINUTES · SERVES 6 TO 8

- 1 (6-ounce) package fresh baby spinach, thoroughly washed
- 1/3 cup refrigerated pesto
- 1 (15-ounce) jar Alfredo sauce
- 1/4 cup vegetable broth*
- 1 (25-ounce) package frozen cheese-filled ravioli (do not thaw)
- 4 ounces shredded 6-cheese Italian blend cheese (about 1 cup)

  Fresh basil leaves, paprika (optional)

1. Preheat the oven to 400°F. Chop the spinach, and toss with the pesto in a medium bowl.

2. Combine the Alfredo sauce and the vegetable broth. Spoon one-third of the Alfredo sauce mixture (about 1/2 cup) into a lightly greased 2.2-quart or 11- x 7-inch baking dish. Top with half of the spinach mixture. Arrange half of the ravioli in a single layer over the spinach mixture. Repeat the layers once. Top with the remaining Alfredo sauce mixture.

3. Bake for 20 minutes. Remove from the oven, and sprinkle with the shredded cheese. Bake 5 minutes or until hot and bubbly. Garnish with the basil and, if desired, paprika.

Chicken broth may be substituted.

QUICK AND EASY SPAGHETTI BOLOGNESE

To create a satisfying meat sauce, cook Italian sausage, peppers, sweet onions, and garlic, and then add a quality jarred pasta sauce. We know what you are thinking: Grandmother would never use a jarred sauce! But if she could taste this recipe, she might just give her nod of approval. Remember to reserve some pasta water before you drain the spaghetti noodles, because adding the starchy water to the meat sauce adds body.

30 MINUTES · SERVES 4

- 1 tablespoon olive oil
- 1 pound sweet Italian sausage, casings removed
- ½ cup chopped sweet onion
- ½ cup chopped green bell pepper
- 2 garlic cloves, minced
- 1 (24-ounce) jar tomato and basil pasta sauce (such as Barilla or Classico)
- 1 teaspoon sugar
- ½ teaspoon table salt
- ¼ teaspoon freshly ground black pepper
- 1 (16-ounce) package spaghetti or linguine
- 2 tablespoons chopped fresh basil
  Grated Parmesan cheese, fresh basil leaves (optional)

1. Heat the oil in a large skillet over medium-high. Add the sausage, onion, bell pepper, and garlic, and cook, stirring, until the sausage is browned and the vegetables are tender, 8 to 10 minutes.

2. Stir in the pasta sauce, sugar, salt, and black pepper; bring the mixture to a boil over medium-high. Reduce heat to low; simmer 15 minutes.

3. Cook the pasta according to the package directions. Drain, reserving ½ cup cooking water. Stir the chopped basil into the meat sauce. Stir in up to ½ cup reserved cooking water, adding ¼ cup at a time, if needed, to reach desired consistency. Serve the sauce over the cooked spaghetti. Garnish with the grated Parmesan and basil leaves, if desired.

KITCHEN SECRET: TIME-SHAVER

Pasta is one of the quickest meals you can make, but there's an easy way to get it on the table even faster: When you're filling your stockpot from the tap, use very hot water to kick-start the boiling process. (Try this to speed up blanching or boiling vegetables, too.)

30
MINUTES

FRIED PORK CHOPS WITH PEAS AND POTATOES

Fried pork chops are a favorite classic Southern dish, and they are usually dredged in seasoned flour, fried in several inches of grease, and smothered in a fat-laden gravy. While we agree that method is certainly delicious, we designed this recipe to give you all the flavors of the classic dish without so much fat.

30 MINUTES · SERVES 4

1 1/2 pounds Yukon Gold potatoes, quartered

1 medium-sized yellow onion, quartered

3 tablespoons olive oil

1 1/2 teaspoons table salt

1 1/4 teaspoons freshly ground black pepper

1/3 cup plus 1 tablespoon all-purpose flour

4 (6-ounce) bone-in pork chops (about 1/2-inch thick)

3 tablespoons unsalted butter

1/4 cup dry white wine

1 cup chicken stock

1 (12- or 15-ounce) package microwave-in-bag petite green peas

2 tablespoons chopped fresh flat-leaf parsley

1. Preheat the oven to 450°F. Place the potatoes and onion in a rimmed baking sheet. Drizzle with 1 tablespoon of the olive oil, and sprinkle with 1/2 teaspoon each of the salt and pepper. Bake until the potatoes are golden brown and tender and the onion is soft, about 25 minutes.

2. While the potatoes and onion bake, stir together 1/3 cup of the flour and 1/2 teaspoon each of the salt and pepper in a small, shallow dish. Dredge the pork chops in the flour mixture, evenly coating all sides. Heat the remaining 2 tablespoons olive oil in a large skillet over medium-high. Add the pork chops, and cook until golden, about 4 minutes per side. Transfer the pork chops to a platter.

3. Melt 2 tablespoons of the butter in the pan. Add the remaining 1 tablespoon flour, whisking until smooth. Add the wine, and cook, stirring and scraping to loosen the browned bits from the bottom of the pan, until reduced by about one-third, about 2 minutes. Add the chicken stock; bring to a boil, and reduce heat to medium-low. Cook, stirring occasionally, until the sauce is thickened, about 4 minutes.

4. Cook the peas according to the package directions; transfer to a small bowl. Stir in the remaining 1/2 teaspoon salt, 1/4 teaspoon pepper, and 1 tablespoon butter until combined. Serve the pork chops with the potato mixture, peas, and sauce; sprinkle with the parsley just before serving.

BEER-BATTERED FRIED FISH

This pub favorite is delicious served with tartar sauce or with malt vinegar (English fish-and-chips style). You can substitute any type of white, flaky fish for the grouper.

30 MINUTES · SERVES 8

Vegetable oil

2 pounds grouper fillets, cut into pieces

2 teaspoons table salt

1/2 teaspoon freshly ground black pepper

1 1/2 cups all-purpose flour

1 1/2 teaspoons sugar

1 (12-ounce) bottle beer

1 teaspoon hot sauce

1. Preheat the oven to 200°F. Pour the oil to a depth of 3 inches into a large Dutch oven; heat to 360°F.

2. While the oil heats, sprinkle the fish with 1 teaspoon of the salt and the black pepper.

3. Whisk together the flour, sugar, and remaining 1 teaspoon salt in a large bowl. Whisk in the beer and hot sauce. Dip the fish in the batter, allowing excess batter to drip off.

4. Gently lower the fish into the hot oil using tongs (to prevent the fish from sticking to the Dutch oven). Fry the fish, in 4 batches, 2 to 3 minutes on each side or until golden brown. Place the fried fish on a wire rack in a jelly-roll pan; keep warm in the oven until ready to serve.

30
MINUTES

ON THE SIDE

Because it isn't a meal without an
ideal accompaniment, whip up the
perfect partner for the star of the
plate from this selection of quick, colorful,
and oh-so-delicious side dishes.

LETTUCE WEDGE WITH SPICY MISO DRESSING

Miso is a Japanese staple with a slightly salty, pungent flavor.
Find it in the international or refrigerated aisle at your grocery store.

10 MINUTES · SERVES 6

- 1 head iceberg lettuce, cut into 6 wedges
- 1/2 cup plain low-fat yogurt
- 2 tablespoons spicy miso teriyaki sauce
- 1 1/2 tablespoons milk
- 1/4 cup matchstick-cut carrots
- 1/2 cup julienned red bell pepper
- 1/2 red onion, vertically sliced
- Fresh cilantro leaves (optional)

Place the lettuce wedges on the salad plates. Whisk together the yogurt, teriyaki sauce, and milk until smooth. Spoon the dressing evenly over the lettuce wedges; sprinkle evenly with the carrots, pepper, and onion. Garnish with the cilantro, if desired.

10
MINUTES

CANDIED BALSAMIC TOMATOES AND MOZZARELLA SALAD

Succulent grape tomatoes are kissed with sugar, splashed with
tangy balsamic vinegar, and finished with mozzarella and fresh basil.
Try any combination of colorful tomatoes when they're in season.

10 MINUTES · SERVES 2

1 teaspoon olive oil

4 cups grape tomatoes

1 teaspoon sugar

1/4 teaspoon table salt

1/4 teaspoon freshly ground
black pepper

1 tablespoon balsamic vinegar

4 ounces fresh mozzarella cheese,
drained and cut into small pieces

1/4 cup small fresh basil leaves, torn

1. Heat a large nonstick skillet over medium-high.
Add the olive oil. Add the tomatoes to the pan; cook
5 minutes or until the tomatoes release their juices.
Sprinkle with the sugar, salt, and pepper; cook
2 minutes. Drizzle with the vinegar; cook 30 seconds or just until the vinegar evaporates.

2. Transfer the tomato mixture to a serving bowl.
Add the mozzarella and basil; toss.

LEMONGRASS-CHICKEN LETTUCE CUPS

What gives this light dish charm is the fact that it's a salad rolled up into a convenient, handheld package. If you want to make a lunch-box version, pack the lettuce, peanuts, and cilantro separate from the filling and assemble at lunchtime.

10 MINUTES · SERVES 8

Lemongrass Vinaigrette

3 cups shredded cooked chicken breast

1 cup matchstick-cut carrots

8 Boston lettuce leaves

1/3 cup chopped dry-roasted peanuts

Fresh cilantro leaves (optional)

1. Make the Lemongrass Vinaigrette.

2. Combine the vinaigrette, chicken, and carrots in a medium bowl. Arrange the lettuce evenly on 4 plates. Divide the mixture evenly among the lettuce leaves. Sprinkle with the peanuts and, if desired, the cilantro leaves.

LEMONGRASS VINAIGRETTE

2 tablespoons fresh lime juice

1 tablespoon lemongrass paste (such as Gourmet Garden)

1 tablespoon chopped fresh cilantro

2 teaspoons canola oil

2 teaspoons fish sauce

1 teaspoon reduced-sodium soy sauce

2 garlic cloves, minced

Whisk together all the ingredients in a small bowl. Makes 1/3 cup

CHIPOTLE TACO SALAD

Smoky chipotle salsa replaces sodium-laden taco seasoning mix to flavor the meat in this popular Mexican salad. And it's ready in a flash. Let the fiesta begin! This salad can serve four as a main course.

10 MINUTES · SERVES 8

- 1 pound ground sirloin
- 1 cup chipotle salsa
- 2 tablespoons water
- 1/4 teaspoon table salt
- 6 cups shredded iceberg lettuce
- 4 cups baked tortilla chips
- 1 cup chopped tomato
- 1/2 cup light sour cream
- 1/4 cup sliced scallions
- 4 ounces shredded reduced-fat 4-cheese Mexican blend cheese (about 1 cup)

1. Cook the beef in a large nonstick skillet over medium, stirring constantly, until browned and crumbly, about 8 minutes. Stir in 1/2 cup of the salsa, 2 tablespoons water, and salt; cook 1 minute.

2. Arrange the lettuce evenly on 8 plates; top each serving evenly with the tortilla chips, tomato, meat mixture, sour cream, remaining salsa, scallions, and cheese.

CRAB SALAD WITH BUTTERMILK DRESSING

Buttermilk provides bright tang and creaminess in this
hearty seafood side salad. Lemon zest lends added zing.

10 MINUTES · SERVES 8

Buttermilk Dressing

- 1 **pound jumbo lump crabmeat,
  drained**
- 8 **small Bibb lettuce leaves**
- 2 **cups multicolored cherry tomatoes
  (about 12 ounces), quartered**

1. Make the Buttermilk Dressing.

2. Pick the crabmeat, removing any bits of shell.
Combine the crabmeat and the Buttermilk Dressing;
toss well. Place a lettuce leaf on each plate. Divide the
crab salad evenly among the lettuce leaves; sprinkle
the tomatoes evenly over each salad.

BUTTERMILK DRESSING

- ½ **cup buttermilk**
- ¼ **cup sour cream**
- 2 **teaspoons lemon zest**
- 1 **teaspoon chopped fresh dill**
- ¼ **teaspoon freshly ground
  black pepper**
- ⅛ **teaspoon table salt**

Whisk together all the ingredients in a small bowl.
Makes 3/4 cup

10
MINUTES

TUNA-PITA CHIP PANZANELLA

We borrowed the idea of the traditional Italian bread salad and substituted pita chips for the bread. It's best tossed and eaten right away to appreciate the crunch.

10 MINUTES · SERVES 8 TO 10

3 cups plain pita chips, coarsely broken

1½ cups chopped cucumber (about 1 large)

1 cup multicolored cherry tomatoes, halved

½ cup chopped red onion (about 1 small)

¼ cup pitted kalamata olives, coarsely chopped

1 (12-ounce) can albacore tuna in water, drained and flaked into large chunks

¼ cup light balsamic vinaigrette (such as Kraft)

¼ cup torn fresh mint leaves

¼ teaspoon freshly ground black pepper

Combine the first 6 ingredients in a bowl; toss gently. Drizzle with the vinaigrette; toss. Sprinkle with the mint leaves and pepper; toss well. Serve immediately.

TROPICAL SHRIMP SALAD

A stress-free, hearty salad in 10 minutes? You bet.
Just reach for cooked shrimp, and dress, toss, and enjoy!
Double up the servings for a filling main dish salad for four.

10 MINUTES · SERVES 8

Spicy Ginger Dressing

1½ **pounds large shrimp, cooked, peeled, and coarsely chopped**

1¼ **cups coarsely chopped fresh pineapple**

⅓ **cup sliced radishes (about 5 medium radishes)**

Bibb lettuce leaves (optional)

Make the Spicy Ginger Dressing in a large bowl. Add the shrimp, pineapple, and radishes; toss well. Drizzle with the dressing, and toss again. Serve the shrimp salad on Bibb lettuce leaves, if desired.

SPICY GINGER DRESSING

½ **cup light sesame-ginger dressing**

¼ **cup chopped scallions**

1 **tablespoon fresh lime juice**

1 **tablespoon Asian chili garlic sauce**

Combine all the ingredients. Cover and chill until ready to serve. Makes ¾ cup

10
MINUTES

FONTINA-PESTO TOASTS

These crunchy, gooey crisp breads are perfect for floating atop a bowl of soup, serving in place of croutons on a salad, or topping with Crab Salad (page 94) for a tasty crostini.

10 MINUTES · SERVES 4

12 (1/4-inch-thick) slices French bread baguette

Olive oil cooking spray

3 tablespoons refrigerated pesto sauce

2 ounces shredded fontina cheese (about 1/2 cup)

Fresh basil leaves (optional)

1. Preheat the oven to 400°F.

2. Place the baguette slices on a baking sheet. Coat the slices with cooking spray; spread evenly with the pesto.

3. Bake 3 minutes. Top evenly with the shredded cheese. Bake 3 more minutes or until the cheese melts. Garnish with the basil leaves, if desired.

BASIL RICE PILAF

With just 8 ingredients yet lots of flavor, this is a perfect weeknight side dish
to serve alongside a roasted chicken or grilled salmon.

10 MINUTES · SERVES 4

2 (8.8-ounce) pouches ready-to-serve rice pilaf

2 tablespoons chopped fresh basil

1/2 teaspoon freshly ground black pepper

1/2 cup chopped scallions

1/3 cup toasted slivered almonds

2 teaspoons lemon zest, plus 2 teaspoons fresh lemon juice

2 teaspoons olive oil

Fresh basil leaves (optional)

1. Microwave the rice pilaf according to the package directions; spoon the rice into a serving bowl.

2. Stir in the remaining ingredients, and serve immediately. Garnish with the basil leaves, if desired.

KITCHEN SECRET: USING FRESH OR DRIED HERBS

The flavor of fresh herbs is generally better than that of dried; however, using fresh isn't always practical. Instead, substitute one part dried herbs to three parts fresh. This translates to 1 teaspoon dried for 1 tablespoon fresh. The exception is rosemary: Use equal amounts of fresh and dried.

10
MINUTES

10
MINUTES

ORANGE-CURRY CARROTS

Cut carrots steam quickly in the microwave while a
citrus-spice mixture adds exotic flavor in a flash.

10 MINUTES · SERVES 4

1 (1-pound) package crinkle-cut carrots
3 tablespoons water
1 teaspoon orange zest
⅓ cup orange marmalade
1 teaspoon curry powder
½ teaspoon table salt
½ teaspoon red pepper flakes
Freshly ground black pepper, fresh thyme sprigs (optional)

1. Place the crinkle-cut carrots and 3 tablespoons water in a microwave-safe bowl. Cover the bowl tightly with plastic wrap; fold back a small edge to allow the steam to escape. Microwave at HIGH 5 minutes or until tender. Drain.

2. Stir together the orange zest, marmalade, curry powder, and salt. Toss gently with the hot carrots. Sprinkle with the red pepper and, if desired, the black pepper and thyme sprigs.

MACADAMIA HUMMUS

Turn up the flavor with this tropical twist on hummus that adds macadamias to the usual chickpea blend. It's the perfect dip for vegetables or pita bread but also makes a great slather for sandwiches.

10 MINUTES · SERVES 6 TO 8

2 garlic cloves

½ cup toasted macadamia nuts

3 tablespoons water

2 tablespoons fresh lemon juice

1 tablespoon extra-virgin olive oil

1 (16-ounce) can chickpeas, drained

Olive oil, chopped fresh parsley, and freshly ground black pepper (optional)

Drop the garlic through a food chute with the food processor on. Process until minced. Add the nuts and the next 4 ingredients; process 1 minute or until smooth. Cover and store in the refrigerator for up to 1 week. To serve, drizzle with the olive oil and sprinkle with the fresh parsley and black pepper, if desired.

10
MINUTES

10
MINUTES

ITALIAN SALAD

No need to cook the frozen artichoke hearts—just thaw and pat dry. Creamy store-bought Asiago dressing ups the flavor quotient with the twist of a cap.

10 MINUTES · SERVES 8

1 head iceberg lettuce (about 1 pound), torn
1 (9-ounce) package frozen artichoke hearts, thawed*
1 (2.25-ounce) can sliced ripe black olives, drained
1 small red bell pepper, chopped
1 1/4 cups large-cut croutons
1/2 cup sliced pepperoncini salad peppers
1/4 cup chopped red onion
3/4 cup refrigerated creamy Asiago-peppercorn or Parmesan-peppercorn dressing
Freshly ground black pepper (optional)

Place the lettuce in a 4-quart bowl. Arrange the artichoke hearts and the next 5 ingredients over the lettuce. Top with the dressing; gently toss to combine. Sprinkle with the black pepper, if desired. Serve immediately.

1 (14-ounce) can artichoke hearts, drained, may be substituted.

SPINACH-GRAPE CHOPPED SALAD

This colorful salad boasts a delicious combination of flavors—and it comes together in a snap.

10 MINUTES · SERVES 4

2 tablespoons pine nuts

1 (6-ounce) package fresh baby spinach

1 cup seedless red grapes, halved

1 ounce crumbled feta cheese (about ¼ cup)

¼ cup light raspberry-walnut vinaigrette

1. Heat the pine nuts in a small skillet over medium-high, stirring constantly, 5 minutes or until toasted and fragrant.

2. Coarsely chop the spinach. Toss together the spinach, grapes, feta, and vinaigrette in a serving bowl. Sprinkle with the pine nuts, and serve immediately.

{

KITCHEN SECRET: GET RICH!

If you like your salad dressing a little creamier, add some Greek yogurt to thicken it.

}

10
MINUTES

APPLE-CRANBERRY COLESLAW

This crunchy slaw is full of seasonal flavors: sweet and tart dried cranberries, crisp and cool Gala apples, and toasty pecans. It's a perfect picnic side.

20 MINUTES · SERVES 6

- 1 (10-ounce) package shredded green cabbage
- 1 cup shredded red cabbage (from 1 small head)
- 1 celery stalk, thinly sliced
- 2/3 cup bottled coleslaw dressing
- 1/2 cup sweetened dried cranberries
- 1/2 cup pecan halves, chopped and toasted
- 1 medium Gala apple, cut into thin strips
- 2 scallions, sliced

Combine all the ingredients in a bowl; toss gently. Let stand 10 minutes before serving, tossing occasionally.

BLUE CHEESE–BACON SLAW

After rinsing the coleslaw mix with cold water, drain it very well to keep the shreds crisp. You can use a salad spinner to do this.

20 MINUTES · SERVES 8

2 (12-ounce) packages broccoli coleslaw mix

1 red onion, sliced vertically

8 bacon slices, cooked and crumbled

1 (16-ounce) bottle ranch salad dressing

4 ounces crumbled blue cheese (about 1 cup)

Chopped fresh parsley (optional)

1. Rinse the coleslaw mix with cold water; drain well. Combine the coleslaw mix, onion, and bacon in a large bowl; toss the mixture to combine.

2. Stir together the ranch dressing and blue cheese. Add to the coleslaw mixture just before serving. Toss.

KITCHEN SECRET: SHORTCUT DRESSING

The gray-blue streaks in blue cheese are actually edible mold that helps provide the crumbly cheese with a tangy flavor. Blending the cheese with bottled ranch dressing makes a tasty and quick homemade dressing.

20
MINUTES

BLISTERED BRUSSELS SPROUTS WITH MINT

This is the absolute best way to cook Brussels sprouts. High-heat searing caramelizes the outside and yields crisp-tender texture inside. Use a 12-inch cast-iron skillet, or work in two batches.

20 MINUTES · SERVES 4

1 pound fresh Brussels sprouts
3 tablespoons canola oil
3/4 teaspoon table salt
1 tablespoon honey
1 tablespoon hot water
1 tablespoon minced garlic (about 2 cloves)
1 tablespoon soy sauce
1/4 teaspoon minced red chile
1/2 cup fresh mint leaves

1. Heat a 12-inch cast-iron skillet over medium-high 5 minutes.

2. Trim the Brussels sprouts, and cut in half lengthwise. Add the canola oil to the skillet, and tilt the pan to evenly coat the bottom. Place the Brussels sprouts, cut sides down, in a single layer in the pan. Cook, without stirring, 4 minutes or until browned. Sprinkle with the salt; stir and cook 2 more minutes.

3. Stir together the honey and hot water. Stir the minced garlic, soy sauce, minced red chile, and honey mixture into the Brussels sprouts. Stir in the mint leaves, and serve immediately.

ROASTED BROCCOLI WITH ORANGE-CHIPOTLE BUTTER

Here's a side dish worthy of the finest dinner menu. Fresh orange flavor and smoky chipotle pepper hit hot roasted broccoli and sizzle with goodness. Chicken, beef, or pork makes a fine partner.

20 MINUTES · SERVES 6 TO 8

2 (12-ounce) packages fresh broccoli florets

2 tablespoons olive oil

1/4 cup (2 ounces) unsalted butter, softened

2 teaspoons orange zest

1 teaspoon minced canned chipotle peppers in adobo sauce

1/2 teaspoon table salt

1/4 teaspoon freshly ground black pepper

1. Preheat the oven to 450°F. Combine the broccoli and oil in a large bowl; toss to coat. Place the broccoli in a single layer on an ungreased jelly-roll pan. Roast 15 to 17 minutes or until the broccoli is crisp-tender.

2. While the broccoli roasts, combine the butter and the next 4 ingredients in a large bowl. Add the roasted broccoli to the bowl, and toss to coat. Serve hot.

{
KITCHEN SECRET: PRO TOOLS
Grate the orange zest over wax paper for easy cleanup. Gently run the fruit up and down a micro grater or the fine face of a box grater.
}

20
MINUTES

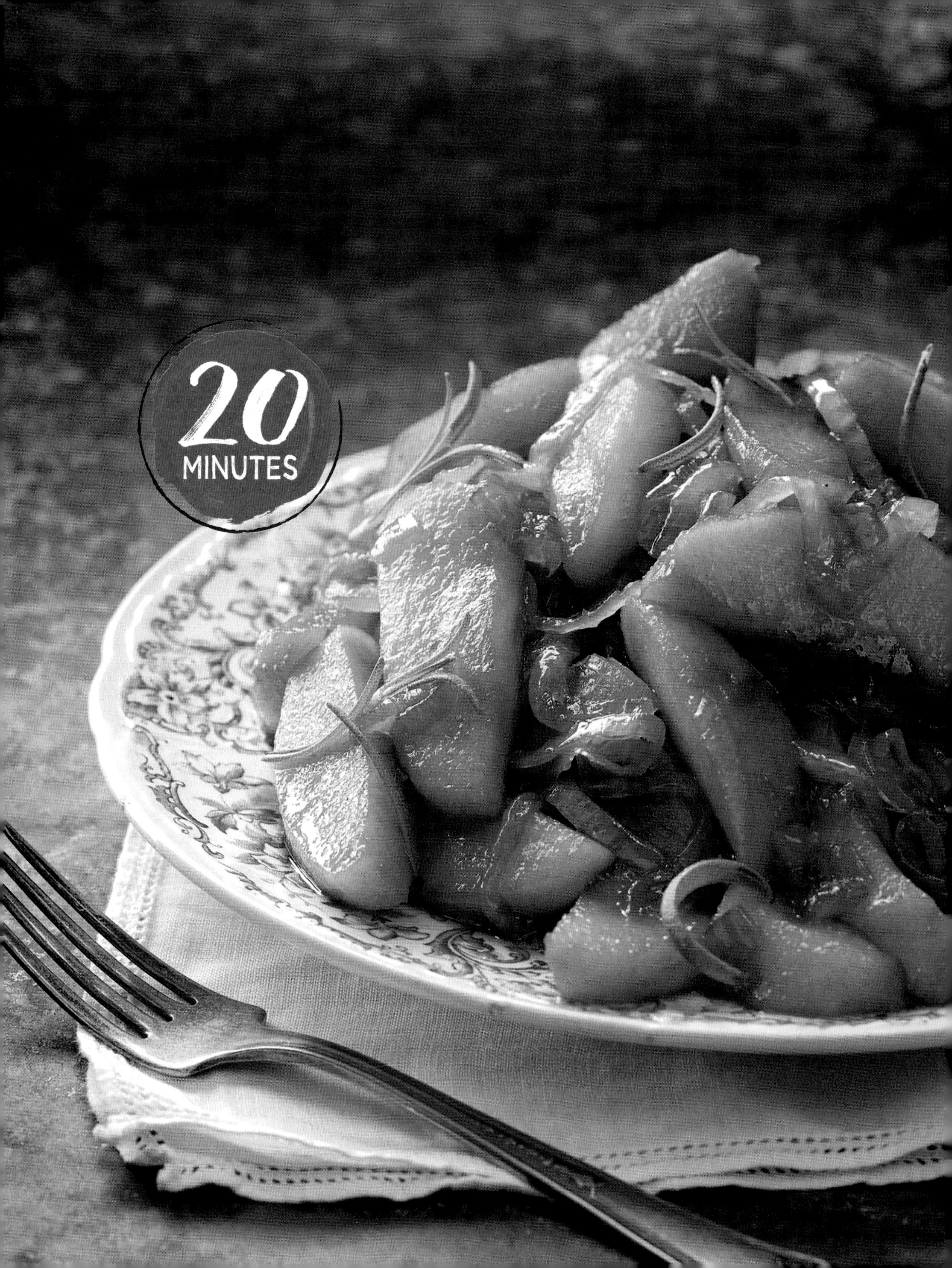
20
MINUTES

SKILLET-FRIED BALSAMIC APPLES AND SWEET ONIONS

Balsamic vinegar and onion give this dish a savory note that's perfect with grilled chicken or pan-fried pork chops. It's also delicious sprinkled with lightly salted, roasted pecans.

20 MINUTES · SERVES 6

3 tablespoons unsalted butter

2 large sweet onions, sliced

5 large Granny Smith apples, peeled and sliced (about 2 1/4 pounds)

2/3 cup firmly packed light brown sugar

1/4 cup balsamic vinegar

Fresh rosemary leaves (optional)

Melt the butter in a large skillet over medium-high; add the onion, and sauté 5 minutes. Add the apples, brown sugar, and balsamic vinegar, and sauté 15 to 20 minutes or until the apples are tender. Garnish with the rosemary leaves, if desired.

CARAMELIZED SPICY GREEN BEANS

This irresistible dish will turn even the pickiest eaters into vegetable lovers. The slight char the beans get in a scorching hot skillet lends sweet, caramelized flavor.

20 MINUTES · SERVES 4

1 pound fresh haricots verts (tiny green beans)

2 tablespoons light brown sugar

1 tablespoon soy sauce

1/2 teaspoon crushed red pepper

1 teaspoon peanut oil

1 medium-sized red bell pepper, sliced

1/2 medium-sized sweet onion, sliced

3/4 teaspoon seasoned salt

1. Cook the haricots verts in boiling salted water to cover 1 minute; drain. Plunge the green beans into ice water to stop the cooking process; drain well, pressing between paper towels. Stir together the brown sugar, soy sauce, and crushed red pepper.

2. Heat the oil in a large skillet over high; add the bell pepper, onion, and green beans, and cook 3 to 5 minutes or until the beans look blistered. Sprinkle with the seasoned salt. Remove from heat; add the soy sauce mixture to the green bean mixture, and stir to coat.

NUTTY OKRA

Pulse the nuts in a food processor for quick-and-easy chopping. Substitute pecans for the peanuts for another decidedly Southern spin on this regional favorite.

20 MINUTES · SERVES 4

1   pound fresh okra, cut into
     1/2-inch pieces*

1   teaspoon table salt

1   large egg white, lightly beaten

1   cup all-purpose baking mix

1/2 cup finely chopped salted
     dry-roasted peanuts

1/2 teaspoon freshly ground
     black pepper

     Peanut oil

1. Toss the okra with the salt, and let stand 15 minutes. Add the egg white, stirring to coat. Stir together the baking mix and next 2 ingredients in a large bowl. Add the okra, tossing to coat; gently press the peanut mixture onto the okra, shaking off excess.

2. Pour the oil to a depth of 2 inches into a Dutch oven or cast-iron skillet; heat to 375°F. Fry the okra, in batches, 2 to 4 minutes or until golden; drain on paper towels.

*1 (16-ounce) package frozen cut okra, thawed, may be substituted.

BBQ BEANS

One taste of these baked beans, and you'll think they've simmered all day long. But they're done in just 15 minutes. This recipe makes two servings, but it can easily be doubled or tripled to feed more people.

20 MINUTES · SERVES 2

1 (15-ounce) can kidney beans, drained and rinsed

1 (15-ounce) can pinto beans, drained and rinsed

3 tablespoons brown sugar

1 tablespoon dried onion flakes

1/4 cup barbecue sauce

Combine all the ingredients in a medium saucepan. Bring to a boil; cover, reduce heat to low, and simmer 5 minutes, stirring occasionally. Uncover and cook 5 more minutes.

KITCHEN SECRET: MAINTAINING A SIMMER

A constant simmer isn't always easy to regulate, especially on a gas stovetop. Even at the lowest setting, the heat can be too intense and cause the liquid to boil. Turning the flame too low can cause it to extinguish. To avoid this, put the pot to one side of the flame, or use a device called a flame tamer or heat diffuser to absorb some of the stove's heat.

20
MINUTES

ROQUEFORT NOODLES

Even those averse to blue cheese will enjoy this rich and creamy noodle dish. The ripe cheese flavor is balanced with sour cream. Don't skimp on the quality of the blue cheese in this recipe.

20 MINUTES · SERVES 6

1 (12-ounce) package wide egg noodles
1 tablespoon jarred chicken soup base
½ teaspoon olive oil
½ cup (4 ounces) unsalted butter
6 to 8 scallions, sliced
4 to 6 ounces Roquefort or other blue cheese, crumbled (about 1 cup)
1 (8-ounce) container sour cream
Seasoned pepper (optional)

1. Prepare the noodles according to the package directions, adding the chicken soup base and oil to the water.

2. While the noodles cook, melt the butter in a large heavy skillet over medium. Add the scallions, and sauté 5 to 7 minutes or until tender. Reduce heat to medium–low, and stir in the cheese, stirring constantly until the cheese is melted. Remove from heat, and stir in the sour cream until blended and smooth.

3. Toss together the cheese sauce and the hot cooked egg noodles. Add the seasoned pepper, if desired.

SAUTÉED MUSTARD GREENS WITH GARLIC AND LEMON

This dish is a fast take on the usual long-simmered greens. Swap out other hearty greens like kale, collards, or turnip greens for the mustard greens if you prefer.

20 MINUTES • SERVES 8

- 2 tablespoons olive oil
- 4 garlic cloves, thinly sliced
- 3 pounds mustard greens, washed, trimmed, and chopped (about 24 cups)
- 2 tablespoons fresh lemon juice (from 1 lemon)
- 1/4 to 1/2 teaspoon crushed red pepper
- 3/4 teaspoon table salt
- 3/4 teaspoon freshly ground black pepper

1. Heat the oil in a Dutch oven over medium. Add the garlic; cook, stirring often, until the garlic is golden brown and crispy, about 1 minute. Stir in the greens, in batches; cook until wilted, 1 to 2 minutes, before adding more greens. Cover and cook, stirring occasionally, until tender-crisp, 10 to 12 minutes.

2. Stir in the lemon juice and 1/4 teaspoon crushed red pepper. Sprinkle with the salt and black pepper. Stir in an additional 1/4 teaspoon crushed red pepper, if desired.

CORNMEAL POPOVERS

Don't peek at the popovers while they're baking—keeping the oven door closed will help them rise.

30 MINUTES • SERVES 12

- 1 1/2 cups (about 6 3/8 ounces) all-purpose flour
- 1/2 cup fine white cornmeal
- 1 1/2 teaspoons table salt
- 1 3/4 cups whole milk
- 4 large eggs
- 1/4 cup (2 ounces) salted butter, melted

1. Place a 12-cup muffin pan in the oven. Preheat the oven to 450°F. (Do not remove the pan.)

2. Whisk together the flour, cornmeal, and salt in a large bowl. Whisk together the milk and eggs in a medium bowl. Gradually whisk the milk mixture into the flour mixture until well blended.

3. Remove the muffin pan from the oven. Spoon 1 teaspoon of the melted butter into each cup of the hot muffin pan; return muffin pan to the oven for 2 minutes.

4. Remove the muffin pan. Divide the batter among the prepared muffin cups. Bake until puffed and golden brown, 18 to 20 minutes. (Centers will be moist.) Serve immediately.

SLOW COOKER
30-MINUTE PREP!

PREP & FORGET

SLOW-COOKER SWEET POTATOES WITH BACON

This sweet-and-salty side could not be easier to prep on a busy morning before a party. Best part? Because it's made in the slow cooker, you're saving valuable stovetop space.

30-MINUTE PREP! · 6 HOURS · SERVES 6

4 pounds slender sweet potatoes, peeled and cut into 1-inch-thick slices

½ cup frozen orange juice concentrate, thawed

¼ cup (2 ounces) butter, melted

3 tablespoons light brown sugar

2 teaspoons kosher salt

2 teaspoons chopped fresh rosemary

2 teaspoons cornstarch

1 tablespoon cold water

½ cup loosely packed fresh flat-leaf parsley leaves, finely chopped

1 tablespoon orange zest

2 garlic cloves, minced

3 cooked bacon slices, crumbled

1. Place the sweet potatoes in a 5- to 6-quart slow cooker. Stir together the orange juice concentrate and the next 4 ingredients in a small bowl. Pour over the sweet potatoes, tossing to coat.

2. Cover and cook on LOW for 5½ to 6 hours or until the potatoes are tender.

3. Transfer the potatoes to a serving dish, using a slotted spoon. Increase the slow cooker to HIGH. Whisk together the cornstarch and 1 tablespoon cold water until smooth. Whisk the cornstarch mixture into the cooking liquid in the slow cooker. Cook, whisking constantly, 3 to 5 minutes or until the sauce thickens. Spoon the sauce over the potatoes.

4. Stir together the parsley, orange zest, and garlic. Sprinkle the potatoes with the parsley mixture and crumbled bacon.

CREAMED SPINACH

This favorite comfort-food side gets a flavorful boost from freshly grated Parmesan, nutmeg, and toasted pine nuts. Try serving it over grits or with cornbread.

30 MINUTES · SERVES 4

¼ cup pine nuts

½ cup (4 ounces) unsalted butter

2 cups whipping cream

3 ounces Parmesan cheese, grated (about ⅔ cup)

½ teaspoon table salt

½ teaspoon freshly ground black pepper

½ teaspoon freshly grated nutmeg

2 (10-ounce) packages fresh spinach, shredded

1. Preheat the oven to 350°F. Place the pine nuts in a shallow pan; bake, stirring occasionally, 5 minutes or until toasted. Set aside.

2. Bring the butter and whipping cream to a boil over medium-high; reduce heat to medium, and cook, stirring often, 15 minutes or until thickened.

3. Stir in the Parmesan cheese and the next 3 ingredients. Add the shredded spinach, reduce heat to low, and cook, stirring often, until wilted. Sprinkle with the pine nuts.

30
MINUTES

SNAPPY PEA-AND-HERB SALAD

Serve this fragrant side with just about any grilled meat; it plays well off smoky, charred flavors. Toss in feta cheese and shrimp to turn it into a main.

30 MINUTES · SERVES 6

2 cups firmly packed fresh basil, coarsely chopped

1 3/4 cups firmly packed fresh mint, coarsely chopped or torn

1 1/4 cups firmly packed fresh flat-leaf parsley leaves

1 (8-ounce) package sugar snap peas, sliced lengthwise

1/2 cup thinly sliced red onion

3/4 cup Lemon-Shallot Vinaigrette

1. Make the Lemon-Shallot Vinaigrette.

2. Toss together the basil and the next 4 ingredients in a large serving bowl. Drizzle with 1/3 cup of the vinaigrette; toss to coat. Serve immediately with the remaining vinaigrette.

LEMON-SHALLOT VINAIGRETTE

1/2 cup fresh lemon juice

1 minced shallot

1 cup olive oil

1/4 cup minced fresh flat-leaf parsley

1 tablespoon honey

1 tablespoon whole-grain Dijon mustard

1/2 teaspoon table salt

1/4 teaspoon freshly ground black pepper

Stir together the lemon juice and shallot; let stand 5 minutes. Whisk in the olive oil, parsley, honey, mustard, salt, and pepper. Refrigerate in an airtight container up to 1 week. Makes about 2 cups

PEACH AND GINGER SLAW

Turn a coleslaw recipe into a special summertime treat with the addition of chopped fresh peaches, pecans, pepper jelly, and fresh ginger. The peaches add a pleasing sweetness to this savory slaw with ginger's zing.

30 MINUTES · SERVES 8

1 cup chopped pecans

3 tablespoons pepper jelly

1/4 cup rice wine vinegar

1 tablespoon sesame oil

1 teaspoon grated fresh ginger

1/3 cup canola oil

1 (16-ounce) package shredded coleslaw mix

2 large fresh peaches, unpeeled and coarsely chopped (about 2 cups)

1/2 teaspoon table salt

1. Preheat the oven to 350°F. Bake the pecans in a single layer in a shallow pan 10 to 12 minutes or until toasted and fragrant, stirring halfway through. Cool completely, about 10 minutes.

2. While the pecans cool, microwave the jelly in a large microwave-safe bowl at HIGH 15 seconds. Whisk in the vinegar and the next 2 ingredients until blended. Gradually add the canola oil in a slow, steady stream, whisking constantly until well blended.

3. Add the coleslaw mix, and toss to coat. Gently stir in the peaches. Stir in the pecans and salt. Serve immediately, or cover and chill up to 8 hours, stirring in the pecans and salt just before serving.

30
MINUTES

30
MINUTES

CREAMED SILVER QUEEN CORN

Silver Queen is a variety of white corn with milky, creamy kernels. It's beloved for its lightly sweet flavor. Don't be tempted to just cut the corn from the cob with a knife. A corn cutter and creamer creates much, much creamier corn. Look for an antique cutter at estate sales—or for a brand-new one made of wood or stainless steel at hardware and cookware stores. No matter the material, this Southern tool makes creamed corn like nothing else.

30 MINUTES · SERVES 6 TO 8

13 ears fresh Silver Queen corn, husks removed

1 cup milk

1 tablespoon unsalted butter

1/2 teaspoon table salt

1/8 teaspoon freshly ground black pepper

1. Remove the silks from the corn cobs. Use a corn cutter and creamer set over a bowl to cut and cream the kernels from the cobs.

2. Transfer the creamed corn to a large skillet. Add the milk and the next 2 ingredients. Cook over low, stirring often, 20 minutes. (If the corn becomes too thick, add more milk until desired consistency.) Sprinkle with the pepper.

BOW TIE PASTA TOSS

Cooked pasta and a heap of fresh ingredients come together
in a vibrant one-bowl meal that's sure to please everyone.

30 MINUTES · SERVES 4 TO 6

- 8 ounces uncooked bow tie pasta
- 3/4 teaspoon table salt
- 1 cup yellow and red grape tomatoes, cut in half
- 1 (2.25-ounce) can sliced black olives, drained
- 1/4 cup sliced scallions
- 3 tablespoons olive oil
- 3 tablespoons balsamic vinegar
- 1 small garlic clove, pressed
- 1 teaspoon chopped fresh oregano
- 1/2 (4-ounce) package crumbled feta cheese
- Fresh oregano leaves (optional)

1. Prepare the pasta according to the package directions, adding 1/2 teaspoon of the salt to the water; drain well.

2. Place the pasta in a large bowl, and stir in the tomatoes, olives, and scallions.

3. Whisk together the olive oil, the next 3 ingredients, and the remaining 1/4 teaspoon salt; add to the pasta mixture, tossing to coat. Let stand 10 minutes; stir in the feta. Garnish with the oregano leaves, if desired.

{
KITCHEN EXPRESS
Substitute 6 tablespoons balsamic vinaigrette for the
olive oil, vinegar, garlic, and oregano. Proceed as directed.
}

30
MINUTES

30
MINUTES

SWEET TEA RICE WITH PEACHES AND PECANS

Don't let the long name fool you. This is a quick and
easy side packed full of sweet, spicy, and nutty crunch.

30 MINUTES · SERVES 6

2 cups sweetened tea

1 cup uncooked long-grain rice

3/4 teaspoon table salt

2 tablespoons unsalted butter

1/2 cup chopped pecans

1 large jalapeño pepper, seeded and minced

1 large fresh peach, peeled and diced

1 tablespoon chopped fresh chives

1/4 teaspoon freshly ground black pepper

1. Bring the tea to a boil in a 3-quart saucepan over medium-high; stir in the rice and 1/2 teaspoon of the salt. Cover, reduce heat to low, and simmer 20 minutes or until the tea is absorbed and the rice is tender.

2. While the rice simmers, melt the butter in a large skillet over medium; add the pecans, and cook, stirring often, 3 to 4 minutes or until toasted and fragrant. Add the jalapeño, and sauté 1 minute. Stir in the hot cooked rice, peach, chives, pepper, and remaining 1/4 teaspoon salt.

QUICK BUTTERMILK BISCUITS

It only takes three ingredients to make quick, from-scratch buttermilk biscuits. Fill the biscuits with thinly sliced ham, if desired.

30 MINUTES · MAKES ABOUT 3 DOZEN

1 cup shortening
4 cups self-rising soft-wheat flour
1 3/4 cups buttermilk

1. Preheat the oven to 425°F. Cut the shortening into the flour with a pastry blender until crumbly. Add the buttermilk, stirring just until the dry ingredients are moistened.

2. Turn the dough out onto a lightly floured surface, and knead lightly 4 to 5 times. Pat or roll the dough to 3/4-inch thickness, cut with a 1 1/2-inch round cutter, and place on 2 lightly greased baking sheets.

3. Bake 12 to 14 minutes or until lightly browned.

FREEZING INSTRUCTIONS: *Place the unbaked biscuits on pans in the freezer for 30 minutes or until frozen. Transfer the frozen biscuits to ziplock plastic freezer bags, and freeze up to 3 months. Bake the frozen biscuits at 425°F on lightly greased baking sheets 14 to 16 minutes or until lightly browned.*

30
MINUTES

30
MINUTES

PARMESAN BREADSTICKS

Refrigerated dough—like pizza, bread, and pie dough—is a big convenience for time-crunched cooks. Embellish it by rolling seasonings or grated cheese into the dough or sprinkling on top before baking, for a signature touch.

30 MINUTES · MAKES 1 DOZEN

1 ounce Parmesan cheese, freshly grated (about ¼ cup)

½ teaspoon dried parsley flakes

¼ teaspoon garlic powder

1 (11-ounce) can refrigerated breadsticks

3 tablespoons unsalted butter, melted

1 teaspoon table salt

1. Preheat the oven to 375°F. Combine the first 3 ingredients.

2. Roll each piece of dough into a 10-inch rope. Brush with the melted butter, and sprinkle with the cheese mixture.

3. Bake 11 to 13 minutes or until golden. Sprinkle with the salt.

PANTRY & CONVENIENCE

Delicious, easy meals are always appreciated, especially when schedules are tight.
A well-stocked cabinet packed with quality prepared foods is the busy cook's tool kit
for jump-starting flavor and saving time.

10
MINUTES

COCONUT-CORN CHOWDER WITH CHICKEN

Classic corn chowder gets an exotic boost with canned coconut milk in place of the usual cream. For the cilantro-skittish, basil, mint, or chives are delicious herb subs.

10 MINUTES · SERVES 6

3 1/2 cups (1/2-inch) cubed medium-sized red potatoes (6 potatoes)

2 (14 3/4-ounce) cans cream-style corn

1 (13.5-ounce) can coconut milk

3 cups shredded rotisserie chicken

1/4 teaspoon table salt

1/4 teaspoon freshly ground black pepper

1/4 cup chopped scallions

Fresh cilantro leaves, oyster crackers (optional)

1. Place the potatoes in a large microwave-safe bowl. Cover with plastic wrap; vent. Microwave at HIGH 3 minutes or until tender.

2. While the potatoes cook, combine the corn and the next 4 ingredients in a medium saucepan. Cook over medium 3 minutes or just until bubbly, stirring occasionally.

3. Stir the potatoes into the corn mixture. Bring to a boil; reduce heat, and simmer 2 minutes. Ladle the soup into 6 bowls; sprinkle evenly with the scallions. Sprinkle with the cilantro and serve with the oyster crackers, if desired.

CREAMY ROASTED RED BELL PEPPER SOUP

Quality jarred and canned ingredients help get this rich and delicious soup on the table in no time. It's great with a side salad or slice of pizza.

10 MINUTES · SERVES 4

- 2 cups drained bottled roasted red bell peppers
- 1 cup organic vegetable stock
- 1/4 teaspoon freshly ground black pepper, plus more for garnish
- 1 (15-ounce) can cannellini beans, drained and rinsed
- 4 ounces tub-style cream cheese with chives and onion (about 1/2 cup)

Place the first 4 ingredients in a blender or food processor; process until smooth. Pour into a medium saucepan. Bring to a simmer over medium–high, stirring occasionally. Add the cream cheese, stirring just until melted and smooth. Remove from heat. Serve immediately. Garnish with additional black pepper, if desired.

CHICKEN PAELLA

Converted rice is a speedy cook's trick for getting hearty one-dish meals ready in a flash. This quick spin on the traditional rice dish of Valencia, Spain, gets a hint of smokiness from the smoked *pimentón*, or paprika.

10 MINUTES · SERVES 4

1 teaspoon olive oil

1 (8.8-ounce) pouch ready-to-serve precooked Spanish-style rice (such as Uncle Ben's Ready Rice)

2 cups chopped cooked chicken

1/4 cup coarsely chopped pimiento-stuffed olives

2 tablespoons water

1/2 teaspoon smoked paprika

1 (2-ounce) jar diced pimiento, drained

Heat the oil in a large nonstick skillet over medium-high. Add the rice and the next 4 ingredients; cook, stirring constantly, 3 to 4 minutes or until thoroughly heated. Stir in the pimiento just before serving.

GRILLED CHICKEN SAUSAGES WITH CARAWAY SLAW

Toasting the caraway seeds releases their aromatic oils and revs up the flavor of the colorful slaw in these updated hot dogs.

10 MINUTES · SERVES 4

1 (12-ounce) package apple-chicken sausage (such as Al Fresco)

4 (1.7-ounce) bakery-style hot dog buns

Caraway Slaw

1. Preheat the grill.

2. Place the sausages on a greased grill rack. Grill 6 minutes or until the sausages reach the desired degree of doneness, turning once. During the last minute of grilling, open the buns and place, cut sides down, on the grill rack. Toast 1 minute.

3. While the sausages cook, prepare the slaw.

4. Divide the sausages evenly among the buns. Top the sausages evenly with the slaw.

CARAWAY SLAW

1 teaspoon caraway seeds

1 tablespoon chopped fresh parsley

2 tablespoons light mayonnaise

2 teaspoons apple cider vinegar

1/2 teaspoon sugar

1 cup thinly sliced red cabbage

1 cup packaged angel hair slaw

Cook the caraway seeds in a small skillet over medium-high, stirring constantly, 1 to 2 minutes or until fragrant. Combine the seeds, parsley, and the next 3 ingredients in a medium bowl. Add the cabbage and slaw, tossing to coat. Cover and chill until ready to serve. Makes 2 cups

PASTA PUTTANESCA

Don't let the anchovy paste in this favorite Italian sauce scare you.
It adds a salty, meaty quality without any hint of fishiness.

10 MINUTES · SERVES 4

8 ounces uncooked angel hair pasta
  Puttanesca Sauce
8 ounces Italian turkey sausage links
  (such as Jennie-O)
3 tablespoons fresh basil leaves

1. Cook the pasta according to the package directions, omitting salt and fat. Drain.

2. While the pasta cooks, make the Puttanesca Sauce. Remove the casings from the sausage. Heat a large nonstick skillet over medium-high. Add the sausage; cook 4 minutes or until browned, stirring to crumble. Drain, if necessary. Add the Puttanesca Sauce and the pasta to the pan, tossing to coat.

3. Divide the pasta evenly among each of 4 plates. Top the pasta evenly with the basil.

PUTTANESCA SAUCE

1 (24-ounce) jar fire-roasted
  tomato-and-garlic pasta sauce
  (such as Classico)
1/3 cup coarsely chopped pitted
  kalamata olives
1 teaspoon anchovy paste
1/2 teaspoon crushed red pepper

Combine all the ingredients in a medium saucepan. Bring to a boil over medium-high, stirring often. Reduce heat, and simmer 3 minutes. Makes about 3 cups

HONEY MUSTARD–GLAZED HAM

A holiday favorite just got easier—and frees up valuable oven space—thanks to your slow cooker. Put savory Honey Mustard–Glazed Ham on your menu. With minimum ingredients and delicious flavor, this ham won't disappoint.

10-MINUTE PREP! · 8 HOURS 10 MINUTES · SERVES 8 TO 10

1 (7- to 7 ½-pound) fully cooked, bone-in ham

¾ cup firmly packed light brown sugar

¾ cup honey

½ cup Dijon mustard

¼ cup apple juice

Orange wedges, red grapes, fresh flat-leaf parsley sprigs

1. Remove the skin and excess fat from the ham. Score the fat on the ham, 1-inch apart, in a diamond pattern. Place the ham in a 6-quart oval-shaped slow cooker.

2. Stir together the brown sugar and the next 3 ingredients in a small bowl. Brush the brown sugar mixture over the ham. Cover and cook on LOW 8 hours or until a meat thermometer registers 140°F. Garnish, if desired.

SLOW
COOKER
10-MINUTE
PREP!

CRISPY SCALLOPS WITH CHILE-GINGER SNAP PEAS

Panko—or Japanese-style breadcrumbs—gives these succulent scallops a light, crispy crust and a delightful crunch. Look for panko on the baking aisle along with other varieties of breadcrumbs or in the international section of your supermarket.

10 MINUTES • SERVES 4

1 1/2 pounds drypacked large sea scallops (about 12)

1/2 cup panko (Japanese-style breadcrumbs)

2 teaspoons reduced-sodium soy sauce

1 teaspoon curry powder

2 teaspoons canola oil
   Lime wedges

1. Pat the scallops dry with paper towels. Place the panko in a shallow dish.

2. Toss the scallops with the soy sauce in a medium bowl; sprinkle evenly with the curry powder. Dredge in the panko.

3. Heat the oil in a large nonstick skillet over medium-high. Add the scallops to the pan; cook 2 to 3 minutes on each side or until browned. Serve with the lime wedges.

CHILE-GINGER SNAP PEAS

10 MINUTES • SERVES 4

3 tablespoons water

1/2 teaspoon grated fresh ginger

1/2 teaspoon chile paste with garlic (such as sambal oelek)

1/8 teaspoon table salt

1 (8-ounce) package fresh sugar snap peas

1. Whisk together the 3 tablespoons water and the next 3 ingredients in a small bowl.

2. Heat a large nonstick skillet over medium-high. Add the sugar snap peas, and cook, stirring constantly, 1 minute. Add the water mixture to the pan, tossing to coat the peas. Cook 2 minutes or until the sugar snap peas are crisp-tender.

HORSERADISH-DILL SALMON

The essence of horseradish in this creamy sauce wakes up the flavor of the fish, which has a medium-firm flesh and rich flavor. Prepared horseradish is grated fresh horseradish root preserved in vinegar. It can be kept refrigerated for several months or until it begins to darken.

10 MINUTES · SERVES 4

4 (6-ounce) salmon fillets (1-inch thick)

¼ teaspoon table salt

¼ teaspoon freshly ground black pepper

2 tablespoons fat-free sour cream

2 tablespoons light mayonnaise

1 tablespoon prepared horseradish

1 tablespoon chopped fresh dill

1 tablespoon chopped drained capers

1 teaspoon lemon zest

2 teaspoons fresh lemon juice

1. Sprinkle the fillets evenly with the salt and pepper.

2. Heat a large nonstick skillet over medium-high. Add the fillets to the pan; cook 3 to 4 minutes on each side or until desired degree of doneness.

3. While the fillets cook, combine the sour cream and the next 6 ingredients in a small bowl. Spoon 2 tablespoons sauce over each fillet.

10
MINUTES

CHICKEN-APPLE-CHEDDAR SANDWICHES

Shards of crisp apple and sliced Cheddar cheese balance sweet and sharp in this flavorful chicken sandwich. Have the deli shave the chicken into paper-thin slices.

10 MINUTES · SERVES 6

4 (1.5-ounce) frozen focaccia rolls with Asiago and Parmesan cheese
Basil Mayo

6 ounces shaved deli maple-glazed roasted chicken breast (such as Boar's Head)

1 medium Granny Smith apple, thinly sliced

4 (0.7-ounce) slices sharp Cheddar cheese

1. Bake the focaccia according to the package directions. Cut the rolls horizontally in half.

2. Make the Basil Mayo. Spread about 1 tablespoon Basil Mayo evenly over the cut sides of the roll halves.

3. Layer the roll bottoms evenly with the chicken and apple; top with the cheese and roll tops.

BASIL MAYO

¼ cup mayonnaise

1½ tablespoons chopped fresh basil

1 teaspoon Dijon mustard

½ teaspoon freshly ground black pepper

Combine all the ingredients in a small bowl.
Makes ⅓ cup

CHICKEN-AND-WILD RICE SALAD

Wild rice can take 45 minutes to cook, but this quick version uses a convenient pouch of cooked rice, so you can prepare this comforting classic from start to finish in minimal time.

20 MINUTES · SERVES 6

1 cup toasted chopped pecans

3 tablespoons soy sauce

3 tablespoons rice wine vinegar

2 tablespoons sesame oil

1 (8.5-ounce) pouch ready-to-serve whole-grain brown and wild rice mix

3 cups shredded cooked chicken

1 cup diced red bell pepper

1 cup coarsely chopped watercress

¼ cup minced scallions

Freshly ground black pepper (optional)

1. Preheat the oven to 350°F. Bake the pecans in a single layer in a shallow pan 10 to 12 minutes or until toasted and fragrant, stirring halfway through.

2. Whisk together the soy sauce, vinegar, and sesame oil in a large bowl.

3. Prepare the brown and wild rice mix according to the package directions. Stir the chicken, the next 3 ingredients, the pecans, and the rice into the soy sauce mixture. Sprinkle with the black pepper, if desired.

SESAME-CHICKEN GARDEN SALAD

Dress a double batch of this light but satisfying dinner with the sesame dressing. The flavors get even better overnight in the fridge, and leftovers make a gourmet on-the-go lunch.

20 MINUTES · SERVES 4

- 1/2 **cup sesame dressing**
- 2 **tablespoons fresh lime juice**
- 1/4 **teaspoon crushed red pepper**
- 1 **(6-ounce) package regular baby or French baby carrots, thinly sliced lengthwise**
- 1 **(4-ounce) package fresh sugar snap peas, halved lengthwise**
- 1/2 **English cucumber, thinly sliced into half moons**
- 3 **radishes, thinly sliced**
- 2 **boneless skinless rotisserie chicken breasts, sliced**
- 1/3 **cup fresh cilantro leaves**
- 2 **tablespoons toasted sesame seeds**

1. Whisk together the first 3 ingredients; reserve 3 tablespoons.

2. Cook the carrots in boiling salted water to cover 2 to 3 minutes or until crisp-tender. Add the peas; cook 2 more minutes, and drain. Plunge into ice water to stop the cooking process; drain.

3. Toss together the dressing, carrot mixture, cucumber, and radishes. Top with the chicken and cilantro. Drizzle with the reserved 3 tablespoons dressing. Sprinkle with the sesame seeds. Serve immediately, or refrigerate up to 2 days.

20
MINUTES

ROASTED RED PEPPER SANDWICHES

Prepare these sandwiches up to 6 hours ahead.
For a heartier option, add turkey, chicken, or prosciutto.

20 MINUTES · SERVES 4

- 1 (16.5-ounce) jar roasted red bell peppers, drained
- 2 garlic cloves, minced
- 1 (11-inch) loaf ciabatta or focaccia bread, sliced horizontally
- 1 cup (7 ounces) refrigerated olive tapenade
- 1 (8-ounce) container goat cheese
- 1 1/2 cups arugula
- Olive oil (optional)

1. Toss together the red peppers and garlic in a bowl.

2. Spread the cut side of the top half of the bread evenly with the tapenade; spread the cut side of the bottom half evenly with the goat cheese. Layer the red pepper mixture and arugula over the goat cheese. Drizzle with the olive oil, if desired. Place the top half of the bread, tapenade side down, onto the red pepper and arugula layers. Cut into 4 pieces.

CHICKEN-AND-BLACK BEAN CHIMICHANGAS

Upgrade your burritos by crisping them in a skillet, instead
of deep frying in oil, to make this cantina classic.

20 MINUTES · SERVES 4

- 1 pound shredded rotisserie chicken
- 1 (15-ounce) can black beans, drained and rinsed
- 1 (4-ounce) can mild chopped green chiles
- ¼ cup salsa verde
- ½ teaspoon table salt
- ¼ teaspoon freshly ground black pepper
- ¼ cup chopped fresh cilantro
- 4 (10-inch) flour tortillas
- 4 ounces shredded Monterey Jack cheese (about 1 cup)
- ⅓ cup canola oil

  Toppings: guacamole, sour cream, chopped tomatoes

1. Stir together the first 7 ingredients in a large bowl. Divide the chicken mixture among the tortillas, placing the mixture just below the center of each tortilla. Sprinkle with the cheese. Fold the sides of the tortilla over the filling, and roll up.

2. Heat the oil in a large skillet over medium-high. Fry the chimichangas, in 2 batches, in hot oil 3 to 4 minutes on each side or until browned and crispy. Drain on paper towels. Serve with desired toppings.

20
MINUTES

SMOKED PAPRIKA SALMON SLIDERS

These small sandwiches pack incredible flavor—and it's all about the rub. You don't need to fire up the grill to get that smoky backyard barbecue flavor because smoked paprika adds that kick.

20 MINUTES · SERVES 6

Smoked Paprika Rub

3 (6-ounce) salmon fillets (1-inch thick)

1 (15-ounce) package slider buns or dinner rolls

2 tablespoons mayonnaise

½ cup packed arugula or mixed baby salad greens

1. Preheat the broiler.

2. Make the Smoked Paprika Rub; rub over the tops of the fillets, reserving ½ teaspoon. Place the salmon on a broiler pan coated with cooking spray. Broil 10 minutes or until desired degree of doneness. Let cool 5 minutes.

3. While the salmon cools, reduce the oven temperature to 425°F. Heat the rolls according to the package directions. Combine the mayonnaise and reserved ½ teaspoon rub; spread evenly onto the cut sides of the rolls.

4. Remove the skin from the salmon, and cut each fillet in half crosswise. Place the salmon on the roll bottoms. Top with the arugula and roll tops.

NOTE: *We tested with Pepperidge Farm dinner rolls.*

SMOKED PAPRIKA RUB

1 tablespoon smoked paprika

1 tablespoon brown sugar

1 teaspoon orange zest

¼ teaspoon table salt

¼ teaspoon freshly ground black pepper

Combine all the ingredients in a small bowl. Makes 2 ½ tablespoons

20 MINUTES

SHRIMP NOODLE BOWL

Flavor-packed and filling, this hearty bowl is company-worthy and easy to double or triple. Napa cabbage has a tender texture that wilts to silky perfection atop the soup.

20 MINUTES · SERVES 1

- 1 (3-ounce) package Oriental-flavored ramen noodle soup mix
- 2 cups water
- 1 scallion, chopped
- 2 tablespoons chopped fresh cilantro
- 1/2 cup fresh snow peas, trimmed
- 6 peeled and deveined medium-sized raw shrimp (26/30 count)
- 1/4 cup shredded napa cabbage
- 1 to 2 tablespoons chopped peanuts

Stir together the flavor packet from the ramen noodle soup mix, 2 cups water, scallion, and cilantro in a medium saucepan. Bring to a boil; add the noodles and snow peas. Cook 1 minute, and stir in the shrimp. Cook 2 minutes. Transfer to a bowl, and top with the cabbage and peanuts.

NOTE: *You can substitute 1/2 cup chopped cooked chicken for the shrimp.*

GARDEN TOMATO SAUCE OVER PASTA

We love this sauce as a meatless meal over hearty pasta.
Or try it in lasagna or layered in a meatball sub.

20 MINUTES · MAKES ABOUT 3 CUPS

1 tablespoon olive oil

1 onion, diced (about 1 cup)

1 garlic clove, minced

1 (28-ounce) can Italian-seasoned diced tomatoes

¼ teaspoon freshly ground black pepper

¼ cup dry red wine

3 tablespoons chopped fresh oregano or marjoram

Hot cooked pasta

Fresh oregano leaves (optional)

Shaved Parmesan cheese

1. Heat the oil in a Dutch oven over medium–high. Add the onion; cook, stirring often, 3 minutes or until tender. Add the garlic; cook, stirring constantly, 1 minute. Add the tomatoes and pepper. Cook, stirring often, 2 to 3 minutes or until the tomatoes start to release their juices. Add the wine, and cook, stirring occasionally, 5 to 8 minutes or until almost all the liquid has evaporated.

2. Remove from heat, and stir in the chopped oregano. Serve the sauce over the hot cooked pasta. Garnish with the oregano leaves, if desired. Top with the Parmesan cheese.

NOTE: *Store the sauce in an airtight container in the refrigerator up to 1 week, or freeze up to 1 month.*

20
Minutes

20
MINUTES

ORANGE-GLAZED TURKEY WITH CRANBERRY RICE

Celebrate the festive flavors and seasonal fruit of Thanksgiving any time of year. Orange-scented dried cranberries stud quick-cooking rice that accompanies pan-fried turkey cutlets.

20 MINUTES · SERVES 4

- 1 (8.8-ounce) pouch ready-to-serve precooked brown rice
- ½ cup orange-flavored dried sweetened cranberries (such as Craisins)
- 2 tablespoons chopped toasted pecans
- ³/₈ teaspoon table salt
- 1½ pounds turkey cutlets (about 12 cutlets)
- 2 tablespoons unsalted butter
- ⅓ cup low-sugar orange marmalade
  Cooked haricots verts (optional)

1. Prepare the rice in the microwave according to the package directions. Place the cranberries in a medium bowl. Pour the hot rice over the cranberries; let stand 1 minute. Stir the pecans and ⅛ teaspoon of the salt into the rice mixture; cover and keep warm.

2. Sprinkle the turkey cutlets evenly with ⅛ teaspoon salt. Heat a large nonstick skillet over medium-high. Add 1 tablespoon of the butter.

3. Add the cutlets to the pan, salted sides down. Cook 1 minute and sprinkle the tops of cutlets with the remaining ⅛ teaspoon salt. Turn the cutlets and add the remaining tablespoon butter to the pan; cook 1 minute. Transfer the turkey to a platter. Remove the pan from heat; add the marmalade to the hot pan, and stir 30 seconds. Return the turkey and accumulated juices to the pan, turning to coat the cutlets.

4. Spoon the rice mixture onto 4 plates. Top the rice mixture with the turkey cutlets; spoon the sauce over the cutlets. Serve with haricots verts, if desired.

TURKEY CUTLETS WITH LEMON-CAPER SAUCE

If you can't find turkey cutlets, buy turkey breasts and slice them in half.

20 MINUTES · SERVES 4

⅓ cup all-purpose flour

½ teaspoon salt

½ teaspoon freshly ground black pepper

1 pound turkey cutlets

3 tablespoons butter

1 tablespoon olive oil

½ cup dry white wine

3 tablespoons fresh lemon juice

2 garlic cloves, minced

2 tablespoons chopped fresh flat-leaf parsley

2 tablespoons drained capers

Lemon wedges, chopped fresh flat-leaf parsley (optional)

1. Combine the flour, salt, and pepper; dredge the turkey in the mixture.

2. Melt 2 tablespoons of the butter with the oil in a large skillet over medium-high; add the turkey, and cook, in batches, 1½ minutes on each side or until golden. Transfer to a serving dish, and keep warm.

3. Add the white wine, lemon juice, and remaining 1 tablespoon butter to the skillet, stirring to loosen particles from the bottom of the skillet. Cook 2 minutes or just until thoroughly heated.

4. Stir in the garlic, parsley, and capers; spoon over the turkey. Garnish with the lemon wedges and parsley, if desired. Serve immediately.

KITCHEN SECRET: BRING OUT YOUR DREGS!

Need a little wine for a recipe, but don't want to open a bottle? Save the leftover wine from unfinished bottles by pouring it into ice cube trays and freezing. Pop out the wine cubes and store in a ziplock bag in the freezer. One standard ice cube equals 1 ounce liquid.

20
MINUTES

20
MINUTES

CRUNCHY PAN-FRIED CHICKEN

A mix of cornmeal and breadcrumbs gives this fried chicken recipe a crisp bite while keeping the inside of the meat juicy. This crispy coating is also terrific on skinned and boned chicken thighs or pork chops.

20 MINUTES · SERVES 4

- 1/2 **cup self-rising cornmeal mix**
- 1/2 **cup seasoned fine, dry breadcrumbs**
- 1/2 **teaspoon freshly ground black pepper**
- 4 **skinned and boned chicken breasts**
- 1 **large egg, beaten**
- 1/4 **cup vegetable oil**

1. Combine the first 3 ingredients in a shallow dish. Dip the chicken in the egg, and dredge in the cornmeal mixture.

2. Heat the oil in a large skillet over medium-high. Add the chicken to the pan and cook 3 to 5 minutes on each side or until done.

BEEF FAJITAS WITH PICO DE GALLO

Fajita seasoning makes flank steaks flavorful. Simply grill the meat and serve it with tortillas, shredded cheese, pico de gallo, and sour cream—all available ready-to-serve from your grocery store.

20 MINUTES · SERVES 6

3 tablespoons fajita seasoning
2 (1-pound) flank steaks
12 (6-inch) flour tortillas, warmed
Shredded Cheddar cheese
1 (8-ounce) container pico de gallo
Lime wedges, fresh cilantro sprigs, sour cream (optional)

1. Sprinkle the fajita seasoning on the steaks in a shallow dish. Preheat a two-sided contact indoor electric grill on HIGH according to manufacturer's instructions. Place the steaks on the grill rack, close the lid, and grill 10 minutes (medium-rare) or to desired degree of doneness. Remove the steaks, and let stand 5 minutes.

2. Cut the steaks diagonally across the grain into very thin slices, and serve with the tortillas, cheese, and pico de gallo. Garnish with the lime wedges and cilantro, if desired.

NOTE: *When using an outdoor gas or charcoal grill, grill the steaks, covered with the grill lid, over medium-high (350° to 400°F) for 8 minutes. Turn and grill 5 more minutes or to desired degree of doneness. Proceed as directed.*

ROASTED SALMON WITH LEMON AND DILL

Light and healthy, salmon's richness is tempered with bright lemon and fresh dill. A dose of lemon pepper seasoning blend ups the flavor ante with the shake of a bottle. You can make an easy side with more pantry and freezer staples.

20 MINUTES · SERVES 4

4   (6-ounce) salmon fillets
2   teaspoons lemon pepper seasoning
    (such as McCormick)
8   fresh dill sprigs
4   lemon slices, halved

1. Preheat the oven to 425°F. Place the salmon fillets on a lightly greased rack on an aluminum foil-lined jelly-roll pan; sprinkle with the lemon pepper seasoning. Place 2 dill sprigs and 2 lemon halves on each fillet.

2. Bake 15 to 20 minutes or just until the fish flakes with a fork.

EASY SIDE: *Cook 2 (8.8-ounce) pouches ready-to-serve basmati rice according to the package directions. Stir in 1 cup frozen sweet peas, thawed; 1/4 cup chopped fresh flat-leaf parsley; 1 tablespoon chopped fresh mint; and salt and pepper to taste.*

20
MINUTES

MIX 'N' MATCH SPRING PASTA TOSS

Using a mix of different shapes of pasta? Add any larger, thicker shapes to the pot 2 to 3 minutes before the smaller pasta. Feel free to veer from the recipe and use up any vegetables that you have on hand. Try swapping out green beans or broccoli for the sugar snaps or 1/2 cup chopped red bell pepper for the jarred pimiento.

20 MINUTES · SERVES 6

- 3 cups uncooked penne, farfalle, or rotini pasta
- 2 cups shredded cooked chicken
- 1 1/2 cups fresh sugar snap peas, cut into 1/2-inch pieces
- 1 cup matchstick-cut carrots
- 1 (4-ounce) jar diced pimiento, drained
- 1 cup diced cucumber
- 3 scallions, sliced
- 1/2 cup sliced radishes
- 1/2 cup bottled Greek dressing
- 1 tablespoon fresh lemon juice
- 1/2 teaspoon table salt
- 1/4 teaspoon freshly ground black pepper
  Fresh dill sprigs, fresh flat-leaf parsley leaves (optional)

1. Cook the pasta according to the package directions for al dente. Add the chicken and the next 3 ingredients, and cook, stirring often, 1 minute. Drain and place in a large bowl.

2. Stir the cucumber and the next 6 ingredients into the hot pasta mixture until blended. Serve immediately, or cover and chill up to 48 hours. Garnish with the dill sprigs and parsley leaves, if desired.

WHITE LIGHTNING CHICKEN CHILI

This chili gets its name because it takes only 30 minutes from start to finish to get this one-dish meal to the table. Don't drain the chopped green chiles or navy beans. Serve the chili with cornbread.

30 MINUTES · MAKES 11 1/2 CUPS

2 tablespoons olive oil

1 large sweet onion, diced

2 garlic cloves, minced

4 cups shredded cooked chicken

2 (14 1/2-ounce) cans chicken stock

2 (4.5-ounce) cans chopped green chiles

1 (1.25-ounce) package white chicken chili seasoning mix

3 (16-ounce) cans navy beans

Toppings: sour cream, shredded Monterey Jack cheese, fresh cilantro leaves

1. Heat the oil in a large Dutch oven over medium-high. Add the onion and garlic to the pan; cook, stirring often, 5 minutes or until the onion is tender. Stir in the chicken, the next 3 ingredients, and 2 cans of the navy beans. Coarsely mash the remaining can of navy beans, and stir into the chicken mixture.

2. Bring to a boil, stirring often; cover, reduce heat to medium-low, and simmer, stirring occasionally, 10 minutes. While the chili simmers, make the Avocado-Mango Salsa. Serve the chili with the Salsa and desired toppings.

AVOCADO-MANGO SALSA

1 large avocado, cubed

1 cup diced fresh mango

1/3 cup diced red onion

2 tablespoons chopped fresh cilantro

2 tablespoons fresh lime juice

Stir together the avocado, mango, red onion, cilantro, and lime juice. Makes about 2 cups

30
MINUTES

BRISKET AND RICE NOODLES WITH PINEAPPLE SALSA

Pulled pork or cooked shrimp can stand in for the 'cue joint brisket in this light and refreshing one-bowl meal.

30 MINUTES · SERVES 4

8 **cups water**

1 **tablespoon table salt**

1/2 **(8.8-ounce) package thin rice noodles**

1/2 **fresh pineapple, peeled, cored, and finely chopped**

1 1/2 **small kirby cucumbers, seeded and sliced**

1/3 **cup thinly sliced red onion**

2 **tablespoons chopped fresh cilantro**

1 1/2 **tablespoons seasoned rice wine vinegar**

1/2 **teaspoon table salt**

1/4 **teaspoon freshly ground black pepper**

3 **tablespoons hoisin sauce**

2 **tablespoons roasted peanut oil**

2 **tablespoons fresh lime juice**

1 **tablespoon fish sauce**

1 **teaspoon Sriracha chili sauce**

2 **tablespoons water**

4 **cups shredded romaine lettuce**

1 **pound warm shredded smoked beef brisket**

1/2 **cup sliced pickled Peppadew peppers**

1/2 **cup assorted fresh mint, basil, and cilantro leaves and sprigs**

1. Place the 8 cups water and 1 tablespoon table salt in a large microwave-safe glass bowl. Microwave at HIGH 2 minutes. Submerge the noodles in the water; let stand 20 minutes or until tender. Drain.

2. While the noodles stand, toss together the pineapple and the next 6 ingredients.

3. Whisk together the hoisin sauce, the next 4 ingredients, and 2 tablespoons water. Combine the drained noodles and 2 tablespoons hoisin sauce mixture in a medium bowl, tossing to coat.

4. Divide the lettuce among 4 bowls. Top with the noodles, pineapple mixture, brisket, and peppers. Drizzle with the desired amount of the remaining hoisin mixture. Sprinkle with the herbs, and serve immediately.

30 MINUTES

ROASTED GULF SHRIMP WITH ROMESCO

This recipe requires almost no effort for maximum reward. Just 10 minutes in the oven plus our special sauce equals tender, juicy shrimp with a kick.

30 MINUTES · SERVES 4 TO 6

1 1/2 pounds peeled and deveined large raw shrimp

1 tablespoon olive oil

1 teaspoon table salt

1/2 teaspoon freshly ground black pepper

Parchment paper

1 (12-ounce) jar roasted red bell peppers, drained

1/4 cup slivered toasted almonds

2 garlic cloves

2 tablespoons extra-virgin olive oil

1 1/2 tablespoons red wine vinegar

1 tablespoon fresh lemon juice

Chopped fresh flat-leaf parsley, sliced fresh chives (optional)

1. Preheat the oven to 425°F. Toss together the shrimp and the next 3 ingredients in a large bowl. Place the shrimp in a single layer in a parchment paper-lined jelly-roll pan.

2. Process the roasted peppers, almonds, garlic, olive oil, red wine vinegar, and lemon juice in a blender until smooth. Drizzle 1/2 cup sauce over the shrimp.

3. Roast 10 minutes or until the shrimp turn pink. Serve immediately with the remaining sauce. Garnish with the parsley and chives, if desired.

BAJA FISH TOSTADAS WITH PICO DE GALLO SLAW

A coastal classic is simplified and lightened by losing the
breading on the fish. The slaw adds a welcome crunch.

30 MINUTES · SERVES 4

4   (6-inch) corn tortillas
    Cooking spray
    Pico de Gallo Slaw
4   (6-ounce) tilapia fillets
1/4 teaspoon table salt
1/4 teaspoon freshly ground
    black pepper
1/2 cup refrigerated guacamole
    (such as Wholly)
2   tablespoons chopped fresh cilantro

1. Preheat the oven to 400°F.

2. Coat both sides of the corn tortillas with the
cooking spray. Place the tortillas directly on an
oven rack placed in the center of the oven. Bake
5 minutes; turn the tortillas with tongs, and bake an
additional 5 minutes or until crispy. Remove from the
oven with tongs, and place on paper towels.

3. While the tortillas bake, make the Pico de
Gallo Slaw.

4. Preheat the grill to medium (350° to 450°F).

5. Coat both sides of the fish with the cooking spray.
Sprinkle the fish with the salt and pepper. Place the
fish on a greased grill rack; grill, covered, 4 minutes
on each side or until desired degree of doneness.
Using 2 forks, break the fish into large chunks.

6. Place 1 tortilla on each of 4 plates. Spread 2
tablespoons guacamole on each tortilla; spoon
the Pico de Gallo Slaw evenly over the guacamole.
Divide the fish evenly among the tortillas, and
sprinkle with the cilantro.

PICO DE GALLO SLAW

1 1/2 cups packaged shredded iceberg lettuce
1 1/2 cups packaged 3-color deli coleslaw
      (such as Fresh Express)
1   cup fresh pico de gallo
1/3 cup light lime vinaigrette (such as
      Newman's Own)

Combine all the ingredients in a medium bowl; toss
well. Makes about 4 cups

30
MINUTES

TUNA CROQUETTES

A tangy avocado-buttermilk sauce gives these simple croquettes fresh appeal.
Serve them with lettuce or on soft hamburger buns.

30 MINUTES · SERVES 8

1 lime
1/2 cup mayonnaise
1/2 cup chopped fresh cilantro or
flat-leaf parsley
1 avocado, mashed
5 tablespoons buttermilk
1/4 teaspoon table salt
1 tablespoon water
3 (5-ounce) cans solid white tuna in
water, drained
1 large egg, lightly beaten
1/3 cup sliced scallions
1 1/4 cups seasoned panko
(Japanese-style breadcrumbs)
1/4 cup (2 ounces) unsalted butter
Butter lettuce leaves

1. Preheat the oven to 350°F. Grate the zest from the lime to equal 2 teaspoons. Cut the lime in half; squeeze the juice from the lime to equal 5 teaspoons.

2. Process 1/4 cup of the mayonnaise, 1/4 cup of the cilantro, the next 3 ingredients, the water, and 3 teaspoons of the lime juice in a food processor until smooth.

3. Stir together the tuna, the next 2 ingredients, the lime zest, and the remaining 1/4 cup mayonnaise, 1/4 cup cilantro, and 2 teaspoons lime juice. Gently stir in 2/3 cup of the panko. Shape the mixture into 8 (2-inch-wide) patties. Dredge in the remaining panko.

4. Melt the butter in a large nonstick ovenproof skillet over medium; add the patties to the pan, and cook 3 to 4 minutes on each side or until browned. Transfer to the oven.

5. Bake 10 minutes. Serve over the lettuce with the avocado mixture.

WEEKNIGHT COMPANY

Just because a dish can be prepared
in a flash doesn't mean it isn't party worthy.
Impress your guests with these delicious
showstoppers that can be quickly whipped up
so you can join the party.

10
MINUTES

BUTTERY GARLIC SHRIMP

Ready in minutes, this quick seafood dish is perfect for last-minute company. When making the sauce in Step 2, whisk in the butter 1 tablespoon at a time—the key technique in making the sauce velvety.

10 MINUTES · SERVES 6 TO 8

1 1/2 pounds peeled large raw shrimp

1/2 cup (4 ounces) unsalted butter

5 garlic cloves, thinly sliced

1/2 cup dry white wine

1/2 teaspoon table salt

1/2 teaspoon freshly ground
black pepper

1/4 cup chopped fresh flat-leaf parsley
French bread baguette slices, grilled

1. Devein the shrimp, if desired. Melt 2 tablespoons of the butter in a large skillet over medium; add the shrimp, and cook, stirring often, 3 minutes or just until shrimp turn pink. Remove the shrimp from the pan.

2. Add the garlic to the pan, and cook, stirring constantly, 30 seconds. Add the wine, and cook, stirring constantly, 2 minutes. Stir in the salt and pepper. Whisk in the remaining butter, 1 tablespoon at a time, and cook, whisking constantly, 2 to 3 minutes or until thickened. Remove from heat, and add the parsley and cooked shrimp, tossing to coat. Serve with the grilled French bread slices.

SCALLOPS WITH CAPERS AND TOMATOES

Pungent capers and diced tomatoes pair well with seared scallops for a fresh dinner. Serve over angel hair pasta to complete your meal.

10 MINUTES · SERVES 4

1 1/2   pounds drypacked large sea scallops (about 12)

1   garlic clove, minced

1/2   cup dry white wine

1   tomato, seeded and diced (about 1 cup)

3   tablespoons drained capers

2   tablespoons chopped fresh basil

1/4   teaspoon table salt

1   tablespoon extra-virgin olive oil

1. Pat the scallops dry with paper towels. Heat a large nonstick skillet over medium-high. Add the scallops to the pan; cook 3 minutes on each side or until done. Remove the scallops from the pan; keep warm.

2. Add the garlic to the pan; cook 15 seconds. Add the wine and the next 4 ingredients to the pan. Spoon the mixture over the scallops; drizzle evenly with the oil just before serving.

10
MINUTES

GRILLED CHIPOTLE CHICKEN

Ditch your plain grilled chicken for a zesty, perfectly spiced dinner instead. Grilled Chipotle Chicken delivers a smoky heat flavor with a touch of sweetness. Try Mexican oregano for extra zing.

20 MINUTES · SERVES 4

Okra and Tomatoes

- 2 **pounds skinned and boned chicken thighs**
- 2 **tablespoons light brown sugar**
- 1/2 **teaspoon dried oregano**
- 1/2 **teaspoon chipotle chile powder**
- 1/2 **teaspoon table salt**

1. Preheat the grill to medium-high (350˚ to 400˚F). While the grill heats, make the Okra and Tomatoes.

2. Place each chicken thigh between 2 sheets of heavy-duty plastic wrap, and flatten to 1/4-inch thickness, using a rolling pin or flat side of a meat mallet. Combine the sugar and the next 3 ingredients; rub over the chicken.

3. Grill the chicken, covered with the grill lid, 2 to 3 minutes on each side or until done. Remove from the grill, and cover with aluminum foil to keep warm. Serve with the Okra and Tomatoes.

OKRA AND TOMATOES

Thinly sliced, okra—a favorite Southern green veggie—cooks in minutes.
Green and red tomatoes add interest.

SERVES 4

- 8 **ounces fresh okra**
- 1 **large shallot**
- 3 **tablespoons olive oil**
- 1 **large green tomato, chopped**
- 1 **pint grape tomatoes, halved**
- 2 **garlic cloves, minced**
- 1/3 **cup torn fresh basil**
- 1/4 **cup fresh flat-leaf parsley leaves**
- 1/2 **teaspoon table salt**
- 1/2 **teaspoon freshly ground black pepper**

1. Thinly slice the okra and shallot. Heat 2 tablespoons of the olive oil in a large skillet over medium-high. Add the okra and shallot to the pan; stir often, 6 to 8 minutes or until the okra is golden brown. Transfer to a bowl.

2. Heat the remaining 1 tablespoon olive oil in the pan. Add the green tomato, grape tomatoes, and garlic. Cook, stirring often, 2 minutes or until softened. Combine the tomatoes and okra mixture. Stir in the basil, parsley, salt, and pepper.

BRAISED SHORT RIBS AND VEGETABLES

This restaurant-quality dish is sublime and requires just 20 minutes hands-on time before you can walk away all day and let the slow cooker work its magic.

20-MINUTE PREP! · 6 HOURS 20 MINUTES · SERVES 8

- 4 pounds beef short ribs, trimmed and cut in half
- 1 1/2 teaspoons table salt
- 1/2 teaspoon freshly ground black pepper
- 1 tablespoon vegetable oil
- 1 (14-ounce) can fat-free beef broth
- 1 (15 ounce) can diced tomatoes, drained
- 1/2 cup dry red wine
- 4 carrots, peeled and coarsely chopped
- 1 medium-sized sweet onion, cut into 8 wedges
- 1 teaspoon dried thyme
- Hot cooked grits
- Thyme sprigs (optional)

1. Rinse the short ribs, and pat dry. Remove and discard the silver skin, if necessary. Sprinkle the ribs with the salt and pepper.

2. Heat the oil in a Dutch oven over medium. Add the ribs and cook in the hot oil 10 minutes on each side or until browned. Transfer the ribs to a 6-quart slow cooker.

3. Add the broth and the next 5 ingredients to the slow cooker. Cover and cook on HIGH 6 hours or until the meat is tender. Serve over the hot cooked grits. Serve with the fresh thyme, if desired.

SLOW
COOKER
20-MINUTE
PREP!

20
MINUTES

TROUT WITH BOURBON-PECAN-BUTTER SAUCE

Trout fillets can vary in size. Generally, one 6-ounce uncooked fillet is the standard serving size. If trout isn't available, try another flaky white fish. Serve with sautéed spinach.

20 MINUTES · SERVES 4

- ¼ cup stone-ground yellow cornmeal
- 3 tablespoons panko (Japanese-style breadcrumbs)
- 4 (6-ounce) rainbow trout fillets
- ¼ teaspoon table salt
- ¼ teaspoon freshly ground black pepper
- 2 teaspoons olive oil
  Bourbon-Pecan-Butter Sauce

1. Combine the cornmeal and panko in a shallow dish; sprinkle the fish with the salt and pepper. Heat the oil in a large nonstick skillet over medium-high. Dredge the tops of the fish fillets in the cornmeal mixture.

2. Place the fish, breading sides down, in the pan; cook 4 minutes or until browned. Turn the fish over; cook 3 to 4 minutes or until desired degree of doneness. Remove the fish from the pan; cover and keep warm.

3. Make the Bourbon-Pecan-Butter Sauce; spoon the sauce evenly over the fish.

BOURBON-PECAN-BUTTER SAUCE

- 1 tablespoon butter
- ¼ cup pecan pieces
- ¼ cup bourbon
- 1 tablespoon light brown sugar
- 2 tablespoons fat-free, lower-sodium chicken stock
- 1 tablespoon light butter
  Dash of cayenne pepper

1. Melt the butter in a medium nonstick skillet over medium-high. Add the pecans; cook, stirring often, 2 minutes or until toasted. Remove from heat.

2. Add the bourbon, brown sugar, and broth to the pan; bring to a boil. Boil 1 minute or until reduced by half. Remove from heat; add the butter and pepper, stirring until the butter melts. Makes about ¼ cup

GRILLED TRIGGERFISH

Freshness counts with a recipe this elemental. We recommend meaty, just-caught triggerfish, but any firm-fleshed fillets will work—just adjust the cooking time depending on the thickness.

30 MINUTES · SERVES 4

4 (6-ounce) triggerfish fillets
Strawberry-Blueberry Relish
2 tablespoons extra-virgin olive oil
$1/2$ teaspoon table salt
$1/4$ teaspoon freshly ground
black pepper
Lime wedges (optional)

1. Pat the fillets dry with paper towels, and let stand at room temperature 10 minutes. While the fish stands, preheat the grill to medium-high (350° to 400°F) and make the Strawberry-Blueberry Relish.

2. Brush both sides of the fish with the oil; sprinkle with the salt and pepper. Place the fish on a greased grill grate, and grill, covered with the grill lid, 4 minutes or until grill marks appear and the fish no longer sticks to the grate.

3. Carefully turn the fish over, using a metal spatula, and grill, without the grill lid, 2 minutes or just until the fish separates into moist chunks when gently pressed. Serve with the Relish. Garnish with the lime wedges, if desired.

GRILLING IS BEST FOR: *Thin fillets or steaks that are $1/2$-to 1-inch thick, such as triggerfish, tilapia, mahi mahi, tuna, swordfish, and trout.*

EXPERT ADVICE: *First, make sure your grill is clean and hot. Flip once, and don't rush. The fish is ready to turn when it releases easily from the grate without tugging or tearing.*

STRAWBERRY-BLUEBERRY RELISH

Sweet berries and jalapeño heat make this a flavorful accompaniment for your favorite grilled fish. Start the relish while the fish fillets are coming to room temperature.

$1/2$ cup white wine vinegar
$1/2$ cup firmly packed light brown sugar
2 tablespoons minced fresh ginger
1 teaspoon lime zest
$1/2$ teaspoon table salt
1 jalapeño pepper, seeded and minced
2 tablespoons fresh lime juice
2 cups chopped fresh strawberries
1 cup fresh blueberries
1 cup diced cucumber
3 tablespoons minced red onion
2 tablespoons fresh cilantro sprigs

1. Bring the first 5 ingredients to a boil in a small saucepan over medium-high; reduce heat to low, and simmer, stirring occasionally, 5 minutes. Add the jalapeño, and simmer, stirring occasionally, 5 minutes. Remove from heat, and let stand 15 minutes. Stir in the lime juice.

2. Stir together the strawberries and the next 4 ingredients in a medium bowl. Add the vinegar mixture, and stir to coat. Serve immediately, or refrigerate in an airtight container up to 2 days. Makes about 3 cups

30
MINUTES

30
MINUTES

CABBAGE, MUSHROOM, AND BACON PASTA

Want to know the secret to creamy pasta dishes? Reserve some of the pasta water before you drain the pasta. When blended into the cheese and the other recipe ingredients, the starchy water helps create a smooth and creamy sauce.

30 MINUTES · SERVES 4

- 4 thick-cut bacon slices, chopped
- 12 ounces uncooked bucatini pasta
- 8 ounces baby portobello mushrooms, sliced
- 1 teaspoon table salt
- 3/4 teaspoon freshly ground black pepper
- 4 cups shredded savoy cabbage (about 1/2 head of cabbage)
- 2 ounces cream cheese, softened
- 2 tablespoons fresh thyme leaves
- 1 ounce Parmesan cheese, shredded (about 1/4 cup)

1. Bring a large saucepan filled with water to a boil over high.

2. While the water comes to a boil, cook the bacon in a large skillet over medium, stirring occasionally, until crisp, about 8 minutes. Transfer to a plate lined with paper towels, reserving the drippings in the pan.

3. Cook the pasta according to the package directions. Drain well, reserving 1 cup of the pasta cooking water.

4. Add the mushrooms to the pan, and sprinkle with the salt and pepper. Increase heat to medium–high, and cook, stirring occasionally, until golden, about 8 minutes. Add the cabbage, and cook until the cabbage wilts and just begins to caramelize, about 4 minutes. Add the cream cheese and 1/2 cup of the reserved pasta water, and stir until smooth. Fold in the cooked pasta, and cook until heated through, about 2 minutes. (Stir in more cooking water if needed.) Divide evenly among 4 bowls, and top with the cooked bacon, thyme, and Parmesan.

CHICKEN BREASTS WITH MUSHROOMS AND ASPARAGUS

Toasted bread is the perfect starch to sop up the tasty pan sauce from Chicken Breasts with Mushrooms and Asparagus.

30 MINUTES · SERVES 4

4 skinned and boned chicken breasts (about 1 1/2 pounds)

1 teaspoon crushed red pepper

1 teaspoon garlic powder

1 teaspoon table salt

8 scallions (optional)

1 pound fresh asparagus

1/4 cup olive oil

1 (8-ounce) package sliced fresh mushrooms

3 garlic cloves, sliced

2 tablespoons drained capers

2 tablespoons fresh lemon juice

1/4 cup loosely packed fresh dill sprigs or chopped fresh flat-leaf parsley

2 tablespoons unsalted butter

4 slices French bread, toasted

1. Preheat the grill to medium-high (350° to 400°F). Place the chicken between 2 sheets of heavy-duty plastic wrap; flatten to 1/4-inch thickness, using a rolling pin or flat side of a meat mallet. Sprinkle with the crushed red pepper flakes, garlic powder, and salt.

2. Grill the chicken, covered with the grill lid, 4 to 5 minutes. Add the scallions to the grill, if desired, and grill the chicken and scallions 4 to 5 minutes or until the chicken is browned and done.

3. Snap off and discard the tough ends of the asparagus. Heat the oil in a large nonstick skillet over medium-high; cook the asparagus, mushrooms, and garlic in the hot oil, stirring often, 3 to 4 minutes or until the asparagus is crisp-tender. Add the capers and lemon juice; cook 1 to 2 minutes, stirring to loosen the browned bits from the bottom of the pan. Remove from heat; stir in the dill and butter, stirring until the butter melts.

4. Place the chicken and scallions on the bread, and top with the sauce.

30
MINUTES

30
MINUTES

CAST-IRON CHICKEN PICCATA

One (cast-iron) dish and dinner is done, thanks to quick-and-easy Cast-Iron Chicken Piccata. Tip: Wait to add the parsley to the lemon juice and capers until just before serving. This step should help maintain its vivid color and bold flavor.

30 MINUTES · SERVES 4

4 (5- to 6-ounce) chicken cutlets

1/2 cup (about 2 ounces) all-purpose flour

1 1/2 teaspoons table salt

1/4 teaspoon freshly ground black pepper

1 large egg white, lightly beaten

6 tablespoons (3 ounces) salted butter

2 tablespoons olive oil

1 cup reduced-sodium chicken broth

1/4 cup fresh lemon juice

2 tablespoons brined capers, drained and rinsed

1/3 cup chopped fresh flat-leaf parsley
Hot cooked pasta

1. Place each chicken cutlet between 2 sheets of heavy-duty plastic wrap, and flatten to 1/4-inch thickness, using a rolling pin or flat side of a meat mallet. Stir together the flour, salt, and pepper. Dip each cutlet in the egg white, and dredge in the flour mixture, shaking off the excess.

2. Melt 2 tablespoons of the butter with 1 tablespoon of the olive oil in a large cast-iron skillet over medium-high. Add 2 cutlets, and cook until golden brown, 2 to 3 minutes on each side. Transfer to a plate. Wipe the pan clean, and repeat the process with 2 tablespoons of the butter and the remaining 1 tablespoon olive oil and 2 cutlets. Discard the drippings; do not wipe the pan clean.

3. Add the broth, lemon juice, and capers to the pan. Bring to a boil over high, stirring and scraping the bottom of the pan to loosen the browned bits. Reduce heat to medium, and simmer, whisking occasionally, 5 minutes. Whisk in the remaining 2 tablespoons butter. Whisk in the parsley. Spoon the sauce over the chicken, and serve immediately with the pasta.

GARLICKY BEEF-AND-BEAN STIR-FRY

Cut costs at the supermarket by rethinking how you buy meats. Here, we use a less-expensive cut of beef and stretch it by adding colorful fresh veggies to the entrée. Thinly slice the meat and stir-fry it quickly to keep it tender.

30 MINUTES · SERVES 4

- ¼ cup sugar
- 6 tablespoons soy sauce
- 3 tablespoons fresh lime juice
- 1 teaspoon crushed red pepper
- 8 teaspoons minced garlic
- ¼ cup peanut oil
- 1 (10-ounce) sirloin steak, thinly sliced across the grain
- 1 pound fresh green beans
- 2 red bell peppers, cut into ¼- to ½-inch-wide strips
- 2 teaspoons cornstarch
- 3 cups hot cooked rice

1. Combine the first 5 ingredients. Gradually whisk in 3 tablespoons of the oil; transfer to a large zip-lock plastic bag. Add the steak; seal. Let stand at room temperature 15 minutes.

2. Pour the steak and marinade into a bowl. Transfer the steak to a wok, reserving the marinade. Stir-fry the steak in the remaining 1 tablespoon oil over medium-high 1½ minutes or until browned. Remove the steak from the pan. Add the beans and bell peppers to the pan; stir-fry 3 minutes.

3. Whisk the cornstarch into the reserved marinade. Stir the cornstarch mixture into the vegetable mixture. Stir-fry 30 seconds or until the sauce thickens. Stir the steak into the vegetable mixture, and stir-fry 30 seconds. Remove from heat. Serve over the rice.

30 MINUTES

30
MINUTES

PAN-SEARED GROUPER WITH BALSAMIC BROWN BUTTER

This is the secret to restaurant-worthy fish: The magic happens on the bottom of the pan, where the fish forms an even, crisp crust. The sauce seals the deal. Nearly any type of fish works in this recipe, but it is easiest with firm fillets that are at least 1 1/2-inches thick, such as grouper, halibut, sea bass, and striped bass. Make sure the pan is hot before adding the fish. Press very lightly with a spatula while cooking for even searing.

30 MINUTES · SERVES 4

4 (4- to 6-ounce) grouper fillets
1 teaspoon table salt
1/4 teaspoon freshly ground black pepper
2 tablespoons olive oil
1/4 cup (2 ounces) unsalted butter
1 tablespoon balsamic vinegar
1 teaspoon minced shallots
1 teaspoon fresh lemon juice
1/2 teaspoon salt
1/4 teaspoon freshly ground black pepper

1. Preheat the oven to 425°F. Pat the fish dry with paper towels, and let stand at room temperature 10 minutes. Sprinkle the fillets with the salt and pepper.

2. Heat the oil in a large ovenproof skillet over medium-high. Carefully place the fillets, top side down, in the hot oil. Cook 3 to 4 minutes or until the edges are lightly browned. Transfer the pan to the oven.

3. Bake 4 to 5 minutes or until the fish is opaque. Remove the pan from the oven, and place the fish, seared side up, on a platter. Keep warm.

4. Wipe the pan clean. Cook the butter in the pan over medium 2 to 2 1/2 minutes or until the butter begins to turn golden brown. Pour the butter into a small bowl. Whisk in the vinegar, shallots, and lemon juice. Season with the salt and pepper. Spoon the sauce over the fish.

DESSERT IN A DASH

The sweet curtain call of any meal is always a treat, but it doesn't have to involve pastry chef techniques and hours of whisking, baking, and frosting. These sublime sweet endings are simple and swoon worthy.

STRAWBERRY-GINGER LEMONADE FLOATS

Though the ginger is optional, it gives these refreshing floats their signature zing. If you can't find sparkling lemonade, substitute fizzy lemon-lime soda or ginger ale.

10 MINUTES · SERVES 4

2 cups chopped fresh strawberries

¼ cup fresh lemon juice

⅛ teaspoon table salt

2 teaspoons grated fresh ginger (optional)

Premium vanilla bean ice cream

Sparkling lemonade

Process the first 3 ingredients and, if desired, the ginger, in a blender until smooth. Divide half of the mixture among 4 tall sundae glasses; top each with the desired amount of ice cream. Spoon the remaining strawberry mixture over the ice cream; top with the desired amount of sparkling lemonade. Serve immediately.

AMBROSIA MERINGUE TRIFLES

To keep this recipe quick and easy, we use refrigerated orange segments and refrigerated grapefruit segments. A drizzle of honey brings just a little more sweetness. Store-bought meringue cookies crumbled over the citrus segments add a nice crunchy texture to the trifle.

10 MINUTES · SERVES 4

1 cup heavy cream
2 tablespoons powdered sugar
1 teaspoon vanilla extract
1 cup refrigerated orange segments, drained
1 cup refrigerated grapefruit segments, drained
1 1/2 teaspoons honey
1 store-bought vanilla meringue cookie
1 1/2 tablespoons toasted unsweetened flaked coconut

1. Beat the heavy cream, powdered sugar, and vanilla extract with an electric mixer at high speed until stiff peaks form.

2. Combine the orange segments and grapefruit segments; divide half of the citrus mixture evenly among 4 (10-ounce) glasses.

3. Drizzle the fruit with half of the honey. Crumble half of the cookie over the fruit in each glass; top evenly with half of the whipped cream mixture. Sprinkle with half of the coconut. Repeat the layers once.

10 MINUTES

SLOW COOKER
10-MINUTE PREP!

PREP & FORGET
CHOC-CINN LATTE CAKE

Have your cake and coffee, too! This dessert starts with a rich cake mix that gets spiked with cocoa, cinnamon, and coffee before it is transformed into a decadent, moist cake in the slow cooker.

10-MINUTE PREP! · 2 HOURS 10 MINUTES · SERVES 10

1   (16.25-ounce) box white cake mix (such as Betty Crocker Super Moist)

1/3 cup unsweetened cocoa

1/2 teaspoon ground cinnamon

1/2 cup (4 ounces) unsalted butter, melted

1 1/4 cups hot strong brewed coffee

3   large eggs

1   (12-ounce) can evaporated milk

1   (10-ounce) package dark chocolate chips

Sweetened whipped cream or coffee ice cream

Fresh raspberries (optional)

1. Whisk together the cake mix and the next 6 ingredients.

2. Line the bottom and sides of a 6-quart slow cooker with lightly greased aluminum foil, allowing 2 to 3 inches to extend over the sides. Add half of the batter, and sprinkle with the chocolate chips. Top with the remaining batter.

3. Cover and cook on HIGH 1 1/2 hours or until set. Remove the lid; let stand 30 minutes. Lift the cake from the slow cooker, using the foil sides as handles. Serve warm with the whipped cream or ice cream. Garnish with the raspberries, if desired.

BERRY SHORTCAKE ICE-CREAM SANDWICHES

This kid-friendly summer dessert idea is perfect for the lake
or the beach because it takes barely any time to assemble.

20 MINUTES • SERVES 10

1 pound fresh strawberries, sliced

2 cups fresh blueberries

3 tablespoons sugar

10 vanilla or chocolate miniature
ice-cream sandwiches

½ (8-ounce) container frozen whipped
topping, thawed

Fresh mint sprigs (optional)

Combine the strawberries and blueberries; sprinkle with the sugar and toss. Let stand 10 minutes. Spoon the fruit mixture evenly over the miniature ice-cream sandwiches. Top with dollops of whipped topping. Garnish with the mint sprigs, if desired.

APRICOT-PISTACHIO COOKIES

If a cookie can be called healthy, then this might fit the bill.
Antioxidant-rich apricots and dark chocolate combine in a cookie studded
with pistachios. A hit of salt really helps the flavors come together.

20 MINUTES · SERVES 10

6 ounces bittersweet chocolate,
 chopped

1/4 cup chopped pistachios

1/4 cup chopped dried apricots

1/2 teaspoon coarse sea salt

1. Place the chocolate in a small microwave-safe
bowl. Microwave at HIGH 1 minute or until melted,
stirring after 30 seconds.

2. Spoon the chocolate by tablespoonfuls onto wax
paper-lined baking sheets. Sprinkle evenly with
the pistachios, apricots, and sea salt. Refrigerate
10 minutes or until firm.

QUICK APPLE CRISP

Crisp and flavorful apples are delicious just as they are, so you do not need to spend a lot of extra time turning them into a dessert. The addition of some light brown sugar, cinnamon, apple cider, and flour creates a warm and welcome treat.

20 MINUTES · SERVES 4

3 tablespoons butter

2 large Honeycrisp apples

¼ cup packed light brown sugar

½ teaspoon ground cinnamon

⅓ cup apple cider

1 teaspoon all-purpose flour

¼ cup maple-pecan granola
   Ice cream

1. Peel and thinly slice the apples. Melt the butter in a large skillet over medium-high. Add the apples; increase heat to high, and cook until the apples begin to soften, about 3 minutes, stirring once. Sprinkle with the brown sugar and cinnamon, and cook, stirring occasionally, until the sugar melts and the apples are tender, about 3 minutes.

2. Whisk together the apple cider and flour; add to the pan, and cook, stirring constantly, until thickened, about 1 minute. Divide the apple mixture evenly among 4 bowls; sprinkle each with granola, and top with a scoop of vanilla or cinnamon ice cream.

20
MINUTES

CHOCOLATE-PECAN BUTTER CRUNCH CANDY

Savor this barklike candy for its ease of preparation and rich taste. And it's light! It's a go-to holiday recipe for gift-giving or an everyday indulgence. Make a batch in 20 minutes flat, and then let it sit in the fridge for 1 hour to firm up so you can break it into pieces.

20 MINUTES · SERVES 16

68 reduced-fat round butter crackers (such as Ritz, 2 sleeves)

1/2 cup (4 ounces) light butter

1/2 cup firmly packed brown sugar

1 1/2 cups milk chocolate chips

1/2 cup chopped pecans

1. Preheat the oven to 350 F. Chill a jelly-roll pan in the freezer.

2. Place the crackers, slightly overlapping, on a separate jelly-roll pan lined with parchment paper. Bring the butter and brown sugar to a boil in a medium saucepan over medium-high. Reduce heat to medium; cook, stirring occasionally, 5 minutes. Pour the mixture evenly over the crackers.

3. Bake 10 minutes. Turn off the oven. Sprinkle the crackers with the chocolate chips; let stand in the oven, with the door closed, 3 minutes or until the chocolate melts. Spread the melted chocolate evenly over the crackers; sprinkle with the pecans.

4. Carefully slide the parchment with the candy onto the chilled jelly-roll pan. Refrigerate the candy until the chocolate is firm, about 1 hour. Peel the parchment from the candy, and break the candy into 16 pieces.

LOADED BITTERSWEET CHOCOLATE BARK

Three types of chocolate make these decadent yet
light nibbles a powerhouse of fun and flavor.

30 MINUTES · SERVES 16

1 (11.5-ounce) package bittersweet chocolate chips (such as Ghirardelli)

1 cup thin salted pretzel sticks, broken

1/3 cup finely chopped white chocolate

1/4 cup crushed low-fat granola without raisins (such as Kellogg's)

1 (6-ounce) package dark chocolate-coated dried plum bites (such as Sunsweet), coarsely chopped

1. Place the chocolate chips in a microwave-safe bowl; microwave at HIGH 2 minutes or until melted, stirring after 1 minute. Stir in the pretzel pieces.

2. Line a greased 13- x 9-inch baking dish with wax paper. Spread the chocolate-pretzel mixture in the prepared dish. Sprinkle the white chocolate, granola, and plum bites evenly over the top, pressing into the chocolate-pretzel mixture. Refrigerate the candy 20 minutes or until firm.

3. Invert the candy onto a cutting board; peel off the wax paper. Cut into 16 pieces.

PUMPKIN-GINGERSNAP BARS

A creamy, fluffy pumpkin layer tames the peppery, spicy bite of ginger in these bars. Cinnamon-sugar adds another element of flavor to the thin cookie-crust base.

30 MINUTES · SERVES 15

1 1/2 cups crushed gingersnap cookies (about 26 cookies)

3 tablespoons light butter, melted

3 tablespoons bottled cinnamon-sugar Pumpkin Filling

1 cup frozen fat-free whipped topping, thawed

1. Preheat the oven to 350°F.

2. Combine the crushed cookies, butter, and 2 tablespoons of the cinnamon-sugar in a small bowl. Press the mixture evenly into a lightly greased 13- x 9-inch baking pan. Bake 6 minutes or until set.

3. While the crust bakes, make the Pumpkin Filling. Spread the filling evenly over the crust. Bake an additional 20 minutes or until a wooden pick inserted in the center comes out almost clean. Cool completely on a wire rack, and then cut into 15 bars. Serve with a dollop of whipped topping, and sprinkle evenly with the remaining 1 tablespoon cinnamon-sugar.

PUMPKIN FILLING

1 cup (about 4 1/4 ounces) all-purpose flour

1 cup reduced-calorie sugar for baking blend (such as Splenda)

1 teaspoon baking powder

1/2 teaspoon pumpkin pie spice

1/4 teaspoon table salt

1 cup canned pumpkin

1/2 cup egg substitute

2 tablespoons canola oil

1. Weigh or lightly spoon the flour into a dry measuring cup; level with a knife. Combine the flour and the next 4 ingredients in a medium bowl.

2. Combine the pumpkin, egg substitute, and oil in a small bowl, stirring with a whisk. Add the pumpkin mixture to the dry ingredients, stirring until blended. Makes 2 1/4 cups

HONEY CUSTARD WITH BERRIES

Balsamic vinegar is a classic with berries. The acid balances the sweetness of the fruit and the richness of the custard in this cup of springtime dessert perfection.

30 MINUTES · SERVES 8 TO 10

1 cup heavy cream

4 large egg yolks

¼ cup honey

¼ cup white wine (such as Sauvignon Blanc)

1 tablespoon white balsamic vinegar

6 to 8 cups mixed fresh berries (such as strawberries, blueberries, blackberries, and raspberries)

Fresh mint leaves (optional)

1. Beat the cream in a medium bowl at medium-high speed with an electric mixer until soft peaks form. Cover and chill until ready to use.

2. Whisk together the egg yolks, honey, wine, and balsamic vinegar in the top of a double boiler. Bring the water in the bottom pan to a light boil. Cook the egg yolk mixture, whisking constantly, 8 to 10 minutes or until thick and foamy.

3. Remove from heat. Fill a large bowl with ice. Place top of the double boiler containing the egg yolk mixture in the ice, and whisk 5 minutes or until completely cool. Remove from the ice bath, and fold in the whipped cream. If desired, cover and chill up to 24 hours. Spoon the berries into the bowls, and serve with the custard. Garnish with the mint leaves, if desired.

METRIC EQUIVALENTS

The recipes that appear in this cookbook use the standard U.S. method for measuring liquid and dry or solid ingredients (teaspoons, tablespoons, and cups). The information on this chart is provided to help cooks outside the United States successfully use these recipes. All equivalents are approximate.

USEFUL EQUIVALENTS FOR COOKING/OVEN TEMPERATURES

	FAHRENHEIT	CELSIUS	GAS MARK
FREEZE WATER	32° F	0° C	
ROOM TEMPERATURE	68° F	20° C	
BOIL WATER	212° F	100° C	
BAKE	325° F	160° C	3
	350° F	180° C	4
	375° F	190° C	5
	400° F	200° C	6
	425° F	220° C	7
	450° F	230° C	8
BROIL			GRILL

USEFUL EQUIVALENTS FOR LIQUID INGREDIENTS BY VOLUME

1/4 tsp				=	1 ml
1/2 tsp				=	2 ml
1 tsp				=	5 ml
3 tsp = 1 Tbsp			1/2 fl oz	=	15 ml
2 Tbsp	=	1/8 cup	1 fl oz	=	30 ml
4 Tbsp	=	1/4 cup	2 fl oz	=	60 ml
5 1/3 Tbsp	=	1/3 cup	3 fl oz	=	80 ml
8 Tbsp	=	1/2 cup	4 fl oz	=	120 ml
10 2/3 Tbsp	=	2/3 cup	5 fl oz	=	160 ml
12 Tbsp	=	3/4 cup	6 fl oz	=	180 ml
16 Tbsp	=	1 cup	8 fl oz	=	240 ml
1 pt	=	2 cups	16 fl oz	=	480 ml
1 qt	=	4 cups	32 fl oz	=	960 ml
			33 fl oz	=	1,000 ml = 1 l

METRIC EQUIVALENTS FOR DIFFERENT TYPES OF INGREDIENTS

STANDARD CUP	FINE POWDER (e.g., flour)	GRAIN (e.g., rice)	GRANULAR (e.g., sugar)	LIQUID SOLIDS (e.g., butter)	LIQUID (e.g., milk)
1	140 g	150 g	190 g	200 g	240 ml
3/4	105 g	113 g	143 g	150 g	180 ml
2/3	93 g	100 g	125 g	133 g	160 ml
1/2	70 g	75 g	95 g	100 g	120 ml
1/3	47 g	50 g	63 g	67 g	80 ml
1/4	35 g	38 g	48 g	50 g	60 ml
1/8	18 g	19 g	24 g	25 g	30 ml

USEFUL EQUIVALENTS FOR DRY INGREDIENTS BY WEIGHT

To convert ounces to grams, multiply the number of ounces by 30.

1 oz	=	1/16 lb	=	30 g
4 oz	=	1/4 lb	=	120 g
8 oz	=	1/2 lb	=	240 g
12 oz	=	3/4 lb	=	360 g
16 oz	=	1 lb	=	480 g

USEFUL EQUIVALENTS FOR LENGTH

To convert inches to centimeters, multiply the number of inches by 2.5.

1 in	=				2.5 cm
6 in	=	1/2 ft		=	15 cm
12 in	=	1 ft		=	30 cm
36 in	=	3 ft	= 1 yd	=	90 cm
40 in	=				100 cm = 1 m

INDEX